Sinatra
...but buddy, I'm a kind of poem

February 2014

Joe —

Enjoy the music of
the poetry + the poetry
of the music!

Also by Gilbert L. Gigliotti

A Storied Singer:
Frank Sinatra as Literary Conceit

Sinatra

...but buddy, I'm a kind of poem

Gilbert L. Gigliotti
Editor

ENTASIS PRESS
WASHINGTON, D.C.

Published by
ENTASIS PRESS
Washington, D.C.
2008

For permission to use copyrighted material,
grateful acknowledgement is made on pp 152-153,
which are hereby made part of this copyright page.

ISBN 978-0-9800999-0-4

Library of Congress Control Number: 2007910183
Publisher: Entasis Press
Washington, D.C.

This anthology is dedicated to all the ladies in my life:
my wife, Martha, naturally,
but especially my daughters,
Cecilia and Celeste,
who seem to need constant reminding that
Sinatra is everywhere.

Contents

Introduction

The Ambient Vocabulary by Which We Live

Sumatra. Martyrs. Mantra. Sartre. While these are just some of the rhymes for "Sinatra" that have appeared in song lyrics from the last half of the Twentieth Century (and we won't even bother with the variety of "Frank" rhymes), they suggest the very rich and diverse contexts within which the singer-actor-entertainer-mogul has been placed. For the idea of "Frank Sinatra" has far transcended the man who, born in Hoboken, New Jersey, in 1915, became, over the course of the next 82+ years, one of the most recognizable stars in the world. "Frank Sinatra" also has surpassed the Sinatra brand of products: his recordings and films, naturally, as well as his tomato sauce, neckties, and abstract art. But neither the man nor his consumer goods are the primary focus of this collection.

No longer an historical figure only, "Frank Sinatra" has taken on iconic dimensions and has become a touchstone in whom every generation continues to find meaning(s). Often as contradictory as the man himself (as described in so many biographies and profiles) – at times harsh, satiric, sentimental, erotic, comic, and tragic – these meanings have resonated with poets for decades, and I've attempted to capture the multiplicity of those resonances in the selections of this anthology.

This fascination with Sinatra is not limited to poets or songwriters. It extends to writers of fiction such as Don DeLillo (*Underworld)*, E. L. Doctorow (*City of God*), Norman Mailer (*Harlot's Ghost*), and Max Allen Collins (*Chicago Confidential*); and playwrights like Tony Kushner (*Homebody/Kabul*) and Bernard Kops (*Playing Sinatra*). In each case, Sinatra suggests a variety of interpretative possibilities – depending upon the particular Sinatra being invoked.

But who was Sinatra and what his significance(s)? The answers, while many, are necessarily incomplete and insufficient:

· an extraordinarily successful recording artist whose hits spanned more than 40 years and remain familiar to each succeeding generation through their play on radio and television, in film and advertising, and at sporting events: e.g., "All or Nothing at All" (1939), "Nancy (with the Laughing Face)" (1945), "I've Got the World on a String" (1953), "I've Got You under My Skin" (1956), "Come Fly with Me" (1957), "One for My Baby" (1958), "Fly Me to the Moon" (1964), "That's Life" (1966), "Strangers in the Night" (1966), "My Way" (1968), "(Theme from) New York, New York" (1979);

· a movie star who hated re-takes and made not a few forgettable films but whose work in such classics as *The House I Live In* (1945), *On the Town* (1949), *From Here to Eternity* (1953), *The Man with the Golden Arm* (1955), *High Society* (1956), and *The Manchurian Candidate* (1962) reveals the range and depth of a first-rate actor;

· a pop music idol whose fame in the early 1940s as "the Voice" caused bobby-soxers to swoon and paved the way for the subsequent pop hysteria of Elvis and the Beatles;

· a singer known for his impeccable phrasing and remarkable song selection, who along with arranger/ conductor Nelson Riddle and producer Voyle Gilmore in a series of classic mid-1950s albums (e.g., *In the Wee Small Hours, Songs for Swinging Lovers, Come Fly with Me,* and *Frank Sinatra Sings for Only the Lonely*) helped create the canon of the "Great American Songbook," and, by taking advantage of the new technology of the long-playing record, pioneered the concept album;

· a vocalist who eschewed the more recognizable jazz techniques of scatting, etc. but was recognized by leading jazz musicians as being a premier jazz singer;

· a musician unafraid to take chances, from conducting classical pieces (1946, 1956) to collaborating with *bossa nova* master Antonio Carlos Jobim (1967) and poet Rod McKuen (1969);

· a show business legend whose escape from the usual oblivion attending boy-singers-grown-old stands as the prototypical career comeback;

· a businessman who became "Chairman of the Board" when he took full control of his career in 1960, and whose Reprise Records and self-produced "Rat Pack" films (with Dean Martin, Sammy Davis Jr., Peter Lawford, Joey Bishop, *et al.*) signaled the death of the old Hollywood studio system and the ascendancy of a new independent star system;

· a husband to four decidedly different wives: the childhood sweetheart and mother of his children, Nancy Barbato (1939-1951); the glamorous movie star and tumultuous soul-mate, Ava Gardner (1951-1957); the 1960s generation gap incarnate, Mia Farrow (1966-1967); and the keeper of the Sinatra philanthropic flame, Barbara Marx (1976-1998).

· a political bellwether who famously switched from FDR-JFK democrat to Reagan republican, mirroring the conservative shift of the mid-to-late-20th-Century U.S. as a whole; and

· a public personality whose reputed mob ties and tabloid belligerence continue to overshadow his decades-long fight for civil rights as well his persistent generosity, which helped raise some one billion dollars for charity over the course of his career.

All of these Sinatras appear, to a greater or lesser degree, within the poems collected here – perhaps displaying his Whitmanesque multitudes nowhere more prominently than in Paul Fericano's "Sinatra, Sinatra," the volume's second poem, a satire with its poetic, pop cultural, commercial, political, religious, and medical contexts. But all these poems (whether inspired by a specific Sinatra recording or film, an episode – real or imagined – from his much-chronicled life or those of his family and cronies, a photograph or a hazy memory, the color of his eyes or his enunciation of lyrics) capture

Sinatra's place in and around our complex and diverse world. From Hoboken to Corsica, from Spain to Las Vegas, from Canada to Georgia, from France to Wisconsin, these poets and lyricists have peopled their work with celebrated writers, musicians, actors, philosophers, politicians, and, yes, mobsters, but, most persistently and importantly, with all of us – the people in whose quotidian lives Sinatra has become intimately, and inextricably, woven.

Aside from the mediated encounters of Sinatra on the radio, television, or movie screen, we also bump into him when we least expect him (as we dress, shop, eat, walk the dog, remodel the kitchen, run away…), and each meeting offers its own revelation. These poems reflect how his music can surprise us with their insight into our determination (Butcher's "Sinatra"), vulnerability (Stone's "Schmaltz"), and impropriety (Norris's "Ignominy"). For just as his classic recordings continue to play a singularly important role in the soundtrack of both our private and public lives, the poets here employ "Frank Sinatra" across the spectrum of experience: mourning, joy, youthful stupidity, the insight of age, anger, sympathy, humility, bluster, the heat of desire, and the chill of heartbreak. One poet, Aaron Fogel, even tries to imagine that (impossible?) someone who has never even heard of Sinatra!

Sinatra ties us to entertainers past (Jessel's "Jolson" and Hathaway's "…Bob Hope"), of course, but also to a younger musical generation (Reed's "Sex Pistols"), as well to as our mothers (Ridl's "Another Reason…"), to our fathers (Suárez's "*Cosas*…" and LaFemina's "Portrait…"), to our Earth (Raptosh's "Neck and Neck" and Kirchdorfer's "Manger Hum"), and even to our Universe (Lloyd's "The Heavens"). Sometimes he's Fame, sometimes Hubris, and sometimes Love, or at least Lust, sometimes a pet (Keelaghan's "Sinatra and I") or the face of commercial pasta sauce (Capone's "I met her…"), but Sinatra's presence in these poems is always a complex concurrence of the sublime and the mawkish, of the idealistic and the practical, of the soul and the phallus. He thus becomes the kinds of unwieldy and uncanny characters we meet on the streets where we live—even as we try our damnedest to simplify and reduce them to more recognizable and manageable types.

But that, of course, is the challenge and attraction of poetry: the uneasiness its complexity demands of us, its refusal to allow us our simplifications. Poetry's music, after all, aims not to resolve the historical record, but to capture a time's competing rhythms, images, and melodies, or, in Jeremy Reed's words from "Lyricist," "the ambient vocabulary in which we live," – not unlike what Sinatra's 1980 collection *Trilogy* aimed at with its "Songs of the Past, Songs of the Present, and Songs of the Future."   For the three-record set, released at a time when none of his generation was deemed commercial enough to release any recordings, was never intended to capture the best or even the most popular compositions of their eras but rather to offer an acoustic portrait of the artist and, in the end, through his careful song selection and remarkable performances, a portrait of ourselves.

Thus, if, by the end of this book, you know little more of the historical Frank Sinatra than you knew before beginning, fear not. For you will almost certainly, thanks to these poets (and Sinatra's inspiration), recognize yourself and your world a little better.

*

I must express my sincerest gratitude and admiration to all the poets who contributed to this volume for their talent and generosity; to my editor, Ed Perlman; to our matchmaker, Mary Collins; to all the other faculty, staff, administration, and students at Central Connecticut State University for their indulgence of my Sinatra thing – especially the English Department; all the participants in Frank's 90th Birthday Poetry Marathon; and my Fall 2005 Honors 210 class on Sinatra and Stephen Hawking (!?!) – especially Peter Breault (for "Sinatra and I"); to Al Masciocchi for all his excellent musical tips and dedicated listener-ship; to Bernhard Vogel, Beverly Elander, and all The-Voice List; and to WFCS, 107.7 FM New Britain/ Hartford and www.wfcsradio.com and its listeners for their support since 1993.

Gilbert L. Gigliotti

Sinatra
...but buddy, I'm a kind of poem

Diane Raptosh

Neck and Neck

Seahorses do it; colliding like interstellar clouds,
they'll hold each other's tails or grip to the same frond
of sea grass and twirl—happy as sheep at a hump of
onions—sidling by each other snout to snout, the male
throwing noises like finger snaps. Like a pair of mixed
breed pups balanced in the back of a fast moving pickup, both of them up from the squidgy mud, they are
stunned beauty wrapped within fish kiss tail-tip to
withers, scales and scurf sent flying. Two dotted and
spiked necks that go on the full length of the body spiral
thus skyward, horse sweat dripping and rising, her
trunk itching for his pouch, cricket-sounds lasting like
vowels from Sinatra, each of them choked up on
necking's angelical cord, which is ancient as brine, sweet
and right as the brain that talks to itself in sleep. Here
and there one has to let go a sea whinny.

Paul Fericano

Sinatra, Sinatra: The Poem

Sexual reference:
A protruding sinatra
is often laughed at by serious women.

Medical procedure:
A malignant sinatra
must be cut out by a skilled surgeon.

Violent persuasion:
A sawed-off sinatra
is a dangerous weapon at close range.

Congressional question:
Do you deny the charge of ever being
involved in organized sinatra?

Prepared statement:
Kiss my sinatra.
Blow it out your sinatra.

Financial question:
Will supply-side sinatra halt inflation?

Empty expression:
The sinatra stops here.
The sinatra is quicker than the eye.

Strategic question:
Do you think it's possible to win
a limited nuclear sinatra?

Stupid assertion:
Eat sinatra.
Hail Mary full of sinatra.

Serious reflection:
Sinatra this, sinatra that.
Sinatra do, sinatra don't.
Sinatra come, sinatra go.
There's no sinatra like show sinatra.

Historical question:
Is the poet who wrote this poem
still alive?

Biblical fact:
Man does not live by sinatra alone.

Jack Ridl

This Is Another Reason to Write a Poem

When Frank Sinatra died, my mother called,
said, "Well, that's it," and hung up. She'd
been one of the sweet-toothed bobbysoxers
who stood in line for hours, looking in
the windows at the diamonds, dresses, shoes
they'd never have. Step by saddle shoed step, she
moved toward the stage, smoothing down her skirt;
tugging her sunlight white blouse, cut close
at her waist, open through the first three buttons;
feeling her way to a wink, that grin, the song.
"When he was young, your father looked
like Sinatra," she told me once after laughing
at "What's a seven letter word for ol' blue eyes?"
"He was cute like Frank. And tough, too." Later,
she took my sister and me to see The Beatles.
The girl next to us broke her seat jumping on it.
My mother tapped her on the shoulder and
yelled, "Don't ever forget." A few years ago, she
went to see Bruce Springsteen and within a month,
had all the videos, recordings, black sweatshirts. She
hung his photo in the family room. She wears a tour
T-shirt to bed. Each morning, before she fixes her toast,
she plays "Born in the USA," or "Tunnel of Love," or
"She's the One." "It peps me up," she says. Tonight
I called her. I had a joke. She told me about her line
dance lessons and how she walks around the lake
with the economics prof. "He's good company.
Doesn't have much." She told me the boy had been there
to mow, and the grass is brown and that the Fourth of July
will be fun because a big band will be playing "In the Mood,"
and "Star Dust" before the fireworks. I told her

our gardens are blooming and she told me the strawberries
were good this year and that she'd invited six people
for dinner next week and thinks she'll make the meal
now and freeze it. It went on like this and then she said,
"That's enough chit chat, love ya, honey," and hung up,
and I knew she'd take a bath, stay up to watch the news, then
walk to bed in her T-shirt with the crossword and a cup of tea.

Ulf Kirchdorfer

Manger Hum

All that *New York New York*
stuff, you should hear it
in the barn
in South Georgia.

There's a young guy
in a cap
that says G,
for University
of Georgia, Athens,
who hums that tune
when he strokes
the back
of his cow
to win a prize
in the heifer class.

Me thinks
the beast likes
your music
too.
Hear it hum:
[pianissimo]:
Mew York, Mew York.
A moon goes up
over Georgia.

Aaron Fogel

The Man Who Never Heard of Frank Sinatra

The man who never heard of Frank Sinatra: he lived
A perfectly ordinary life in America. Born in 1915,
He followed all the fads, read the newspapers, listened

To television, knew who Dean Martin and Sammy
                              What'shisname
Were (Sinatra's friends), but somehow, by a one in a
Zillion fluke, whenever Sinatra came up, he was out of
                              the room.

Or his attention was diverted by something else, and
(You will say this is impossible, that it cannot be), never
Heard him sing, like a man in my generation who somehow

Missed the Beatles though he had heard everything else.
Once, just as he was about to hear the name Frank Sinatra
A plane flew overhead – he was fifty-five years old – his
                              hearing

A little more impaired. He had heard of Humphrey Bogart,
Of Elizabeth Taylor, of Walter Cronkite, and of perhaps a
                              hundred
Forty thousand other celebrities' names by the time he died,

And yet he had never heard of Frank Sinatra. The Greeks
                              had
That famous saying, "The luckiest man is he who was
                              never born."
Which is kind of gloomy, but I think they were wrong.

The luckiest man is he who never heard of Frank Sinatra.

Jacques Duvall and Alain Chamfort

Sinatra

Björk et Bowie sont à toi
Tom Waits, Lou Reed, Nirvana
Peu d'fautes de goût dans tout ça

Tu t'en vas
Avec tes CDs sous le bras
Mais Sinatra reste là
Sinatra est à moi

Etienne Daho est à toi
Miossec et Dominique A
J'pourrais tous êt'leur papa

Tu t'en vas
Tu reprends tout c'qui est à toi
Mais Sinatra n'y touche pas
Sinatra est à moi

Les Pet Shop Boys sont à toi
Air, les Daft punk, Madonna
T'as l'cœur à danser, moi pas

Tu t'en vas
D'un pas léger, dans la joie
Mais Sinatra, j'plaisante pas
Sinatra est à moi

Chamfort, il était à toi
Mais tu m'le laisses, c'est sympa
C'que j'vais en faire, je sais pas

Tu t'en vas
Tu fais le vide derrière toi
Il me reste plus qu'Sinatra
Sinatra est à moi

Jacques Duvall and Alain Chamfort

Sinatra

translated by Laurence Petit

Björk and Bowie are yours
As well as Tom Waits, Lou Reed and Nirvana
Few poor choices in all that

You're leaving
With your CDs tucked under your arm
But Sinatra's staying
Sinatra's mine

Etienne Daho is yours
As well as Miossec and Dominique A
I could be their father

You're leaving
Taking back all that's yours
But don't touch Sinatra
Sinatra's mine

The Pet Shop Boys are yours
As well as Air, Daft Punk and Madonna
You feel like dancing, I don't

You're leaving
Light-hearted and cheerful
But Sinatra, I'm not kidding
Sinatra's mine

Chamfort was yours
But you're leaving him to me, that's nice
What I'm going to do with him, I don't know

You're leaving
Wiping the slate clean
All I have left's Sinatra
Sinatra's mine

Jeremy Reed

The Sex Pistols

The nihil. And annihilate
the stage we're playing on, the plutocrats
in imported pink Cadillacs,
record emporias. It's anarchy
this war on ourselves and the audience.
We're Fascist Dada. Play to kill

and issue body bags. This club's a barn
packed to ignition, and when I convulse
it's really epilepsy. Sid's back there
so out of it on smack, he wouldn't know

if he was underwater. We can't play,
we're here to lacerate ourselves
in a blood-letting ritual.
I did it my way. Not like Sinatra's

vacuous insincerity,
his words embalmed in acacia-honey.
Mine come out like the points of nails,
a twisted, shrieking, heckler's wail,
hysterical trajectory.
Our venom scorches. We're not here to stay.

George Gerdes

Obituary

Songwriter, Joe Reissler,
often called "Mr. Showbusiness" by folks that knew him
closely,
was killed today by a Mack truck in Elizabeth, New
Jersey.
Joe wrote such old favorites as
"Mama's Got Me Drunk," "Don't Kiss My Feet"
and
"I Wish I was in Copenhagen."
Sid Reissler, co-writer of many of Joe's hits,
commented on his brother's passing by remarking,
"His face was a mess" and "The truck was covered with
blood."

Notables such as Pop Sweeney, owner of Sweeney's
Delicatessen,
were on hand to view the remains
and collect various debts that Joe had mounted.
Frank Sinatra, who once met Joe back in 1943,
summed up Reissler's entire career by remarking,
"Who's he?"

Ruth Moon Kempher

Fabulous Birds, The Rocs, etc.

Long time since Eden came this Roc
Arabic and enormous. Now extinct
I think.

Galloped and flew, but clumsily
its feathers curled like silver bedsprings
on wings

that stretched across a city block.
One flop, and it knocked down any flimsily-
constructed chimney.

Shoddy pagodas, gone. Tiles blew off rooftops.
Storks were smashed in their nests.
We regret

the passing of the Roc. No nimbly
hopping Phoenix from its ashes
at all matches

the Roc. And anyway, they
(Phoenixes) are passé.
Now one dreams of Santa Claus, *et cetera*

or of scrambling eggs for Frank Sinatra
but unfortunately not
of Rocs.

James Keelaghan

Sinatra and I

I have to admit there's a strange tale between us
A twisted road winding between you and I
I was living in a garret on the edges of Staten
I was lying in bed looking out at the night
The gray sky exploded and fire rained down
Some refinery in Jersey had burned to the ground
Call me superstitious I called it a sign
I packed up the van and headed out for the line

I wandered for months it was gorgeous but somehow
I didn't know what I was trying to find
The last days of summer found me crossing the border
I was feeling quite lonely quite out of my mind
I stopped in Regina my spirits were low
If I didn't do something I was bound to explode
If I was gonna keep traveling I needed a date
Rolled the van to a stop at SPCA

There you sat curled up
Back in the corner
Face like a bandit and icy blue eyes
They opened the gate
You casually strolled
Out of the kennel and into my life

So it was that Sinatra and I went a-rovin'
That's what I called him because of his eyes
Turns out as well he's a pretty good singer
Though he tends more to blues than to strangers at night
Old Blue Eyes beside me we kept heading north
Near Whitehorse the van finally gave up the ghost
Got a job in a café where Sinatra begged scraps
We're saving our money for sparkplugs and maps

Some nights when we have both got cabin fever
We'll go for a walk old Sinatra and I
His nose on the ground sniffing out possibilities
Me looking up to the dome of the sky
I'd ask him to sit but he'd pay me no mind
He'll do it his way and I'll do it mine
That's why I like him and what's more that's why
I think there's a future for Sinatra and I

Greg Rappleye

Last Walk with Sinatra's Dog

The Odyssey
Book 11, lines 138-157

Sinatra rises while Barbara is still asleep,
snaps the leash onto Satchmo's collar,
picks up the oar he's kept in the garage
and steps out into the desert.
At first, Satchmo mouths the lead, tail
wagging, eager for a walk.
But as they go beyond the curvy drives,
beyond the last of the flat-footed architecture,
the dog drops the leash,
from time-to-time balancing on three legs
to mark the trail. He looks back
and smiles a doggy-smile: *The years together,*
after so many years apart. The sun arcs
into a cloudless sky, and Sinatra
pulls out a pair of shades. His breath
is labored. He begins to sweat.
But he shifts the oar and walks on,
Until the golf courses and condos
Straggle into nothingness. He slows
Among the jacaranda and mesquite
and looks back. The horizon blurs—
sea-like, oceanic, though there's no sea
but the Salton Sea, vast saline relic
of the orange groves and water-schemes,
there somewhere in the distance.
Sinatra lays down the oar
and begins piling stones around it.
He works slowly, propping it up,
until the oar rises, blade against the sky,
the oar of a boat he rowed as a child,
skimming the mussel flats of Hoboken.

He lights a cigarette and thinks of the lost.
No more *Sinatra looks deeply into her eyes*.
Never again *Sinatra takes a final sip
and moves to center stage*. He begins
a Johnny Mercer song, as he picks up
the lead and pats the dog. *Sky lark,*
he sings, *have you anything to say to me?*
And Satchmo joins in, moaning sadly on
the exhale, as they resume the long walk,
back down the valley
toward the house in Palm Springs.

Ruth E. Foley

Skylark

Eliza sat in silence in the dark,
a cigarette forgotten in her hand.
She listened to Sinatra sing Skylark

again, again. She used the dying spark
of each smoke for the next one. Understand —
Eliza sat in silence in the dark,

but not by choice. She liked to watch the arc
of embers falling floorward. Fire fanned,
she listened to Sinatra sing Skylark.

A thoughtless friend, her husband's harsh remark,
a chore undone, or anything else, and
Eliza sat in silence in the dark

again, again. She cleared the room out, stark
save for the record player on its stand.
She listened to Sinatra sing Skylark

while carpet cracked and burned like brittle bark,
like she did. Whiskey-numb, the way she planned,
Eliza sat in silence in the dark.
She listened to Sinatra sing Skylark.

Kelly Neill

Hang Sinatra

i want to cry
but i don't do that anymore
there's not enough gin left in me
to get strung out
i'm just here
remembering the tears
and forgetting what forgiveness is about
i go around and around
on the wheel of your whim
i want to end this
but i don't know where to start
wondering what miracle of sin
would put some faith back
in a mercenary heart

you used to tell me
that we were cut out just the same
can i face myself
and say it isn't true
wanted dead
who said what and what was said

when neither one of us is certain
which is who
yeah you know me
and i get bored easily
i'll fall asleep on this
before i fall apart
tuck me in and never mind the violins
playing what we wouldn't dare to
in the dark

take the moon down
save the flowers
hang sinatra

Beckian Fritz Goldberg

Walking in the Solstice

Tonight no one makes love. Genie silhouettes
of women float, their B-movie negligees
    skimming screens
among the motels half-lit and wholly quiet.
Suddenly I am the stranger following
cigarettes
down avenues in the innocence of suburbs,
    the cat
who walks with the warp of evening mist
    through parking lots
and elm frazzle to lie in the toy tropic of lawns.

I don't take anyone with me, not even to hear
the radios throw whistles of Sinatra, Tormé.
Nothing I'd do would make one bed groan
under the moon-dumped roofs, or move
    the young men whose
mouths lie tented under newspapers. Tonight
    they don't
hear the junk rain of car keys, or gun for curves.
There is time to learn by heart along the way
the sudden graveyard
of the drive-in, the lunar funk of a living room
where a man sets his dinner tray before
John Wayne. A girl in a second story
    undresses
to the eunuch in the mirror. No complaints.
Just for tonight the need goes away. It is all
in perspective: The housewife is dreaming of
    Aristotle,
the salesman lying down with his shoes.
    And the sulfurous
green-blue of the night horizon
is crowded with blacknesses like boats.

Ruth Stone

Schmaltz

Those rented rooms,
borrowed beds,
when I would lie down
with my length slack against yours
and feel those simple wounds
of the surfaces
with no thought of the garrote.
And here, after all these years,
I am still thinking
if only one more time,
that ordinary naked touch,
unconscious of its death.
And then, this morning,
the shock of an old song,
after the usual trash of the news;
schmaltz, from the big band days;
and Sinatra, of course,
on a scratched record,
the local radio's nostalgia.
It is brief, but for a moment
my body shakes
with the remembered tremor
of your voice.
And then, the aftershock:
that he could bring it back –
this grief for which there is no cure.

Grace Butcher

Sinatra

I was too young or something,
and never a screamer. Tended to like
my family's choice of crooner: Bing,
who made every Christmas a white one
whether it was or not. I never understood
the newsreels of those shrieking, fainting girls
around the bandstand where that skinny guy
with the greasy looking hair swayed with the microphone
and sang (not too well, I thought, even then).

He was still vague to me when he hung out
in Vegas with those guys and did his thing
on stage, always, I swear, off key,
and only that movie saved him in my eyes,
Maggio, moving in the shadows, dark and small,
intense behind the brilliant Burt and Deborah,
their classic kiss, the throbbing, lapping waves.

When Frank got fat and lost a lot of hair
and still kept on performing, straining for
those high notes he never made in the past either,
I thought of him even less, thought less of him.
Ol' Blue Eyes. I never seemed to have a clue
what made him who he was. Never cared.

But funny. Once on my way to wherever, car radio on,
"My Way" suddenly opened me and let him in.
How did he know I always did things his way,
my way, never mind what or who. I had a road to follow.
Funny how he showed up, uninvited, came along,
just a voice singing the right words,
making a road map out of a song.

Kathleen Norris

The Ignominy of the Living

The undertaker had placed pink netting
around your face. I removed it
and gave you a small bouquet, encumbering you
into eternity. "Impedimenta," I hear you say,
scornfully, the way you said it at Penn Station
when we struggled to put your bag onto a contraption
of cords and wheels. "Laurel and Hardy got paid for this,"
I said the third time it fell off,
narrowly missing my foot.

You would have laughed
at the place we brought you to, the hush of carpet,
violins sliding through "The Way We Were,"
"Please turn the music off," I said, civilly,
to the undertaker's assistant.
We had an open grave—no artificial turf—
and your friends lowered you into the ground.

Once you dreamed your mother sweeping
an earthen floor
in a dark, low-ceilinged room.
I see her now: I, too, want to run.
And the "ignominy of the living,"
words you nearly spat out
when one of your beloved dead
was ill-remembered; I thought of that
as I removed the netting.

Today I passed St. Mary's
as the Angelus sounded.
You would have liked that, the ancient practice
in the prairie town not a hundred years old,
the world careering disastrously toward the twenty-first
        century.
I stopped and prayed for you.
Then a recording of "My Way" came scratching out
on the electronic carillon.
"Oh, hell," I said,
and prayed for Frank Sinatra, too.

Robert Wrigley

Sinatra

That skinny fuck-up, all recklessness and bones,
the one your father called feisty, was Prewitt
in the movie, and in your twelve-year-old conception
of things, in the magical drive-in dark, you knew it
was true: you'd found the man you'd aim to
be. Five years later, still confused
by the cinemascope hokum, it was him, not you
screaming at the nightclub bouncer, the fake ID you'd used
slipped neatly into his pocket. Tonight, twenty years
farther into your lives, Sinatra and you have both outlived
those early places. The drive-ins are gone, and Gaslight Square,
and maybe even that bouncer, who shoved
you twice, out the door and against the front wall,
and hit you once so hard in the gut
that you knelt among the sidewalk crowd and cried, all
the night's easy beers boiling out.
There are whole weeks now
when you're trapped inside the stereo's thrall,
when the old Sinatra convincingly sings how
love goes wrong. A little light turns the walls
golden, there's solitaire, whiskey, and comfort,
but you wake up empty. Daydreams run
your life now, and you wonder what sort
of man you might've been, what sort you've become.

Bruce Taylor

Frank
"You make me feel so young."

He tries to act like twenty-two
all sap and spastic charm
when he's around you
it works, he thinks, but then

someone in a barroom mirror
does an ugly double take
and there's that forty year
old fat guy on the make

again, that froggy clown
that roly poly Romeo,
that snaggle toothed Don Juan,
that sad and sleepy Cyrano

to your Juliet, jejune,
your Isolde as ivory ingenue
in waiting to the moon,
ever renewing and ever renewed.

"I'd even be forty for you,"
you say with exaggerated dread,
but by then he'd be sixty-two
and unconcerned, perhaps, or dead.

Of what exactly should he inform
your beautiful youth
almost ever eager in his arms?
Certainly not the truth

which is it's not he is
too old to play this part
but that by now he is,
or ought to be, too smart.

So he plans to leave, maybe,
walk off alone out into the cold,
right after "One for my Baby,
and One More for the Road."

March 16

The weather is on a lottery
system and I've lucked out two
Saturdays in a row it's warm
in Tampa where I want to eat
paella and smoke a cigar and
wonder if Tampax was invented
here I remember the year
my favorite song was "All of Me"
by Sinatra the phrase on everyone's
lips was "in your face" I wrote
odes to the nudes in Lee Friedlander's
photos the tropical tufts of pubic
hair and cheap alarm clocks
constantly going off as if time
were speeding up and the cabdriver
taking me to the airport said
I know you you're the guy who
played the doctor on *Love Boat*

Sam Pereira

Swagger with Microphone, 1963

I keep coming back
To him—Sinatra,
I mean. Every time
A new line comes
My way, I imagine

Frank, cigarette hanging,
And little finger and
Thumb wrapped around
His rocks glass. Frank
Would then swagger,

Holding the black
Microphone and flicking
Its long cord. They had
A cord in those days.
It would be just

About this time, one
Delicious sip of Jack
Into the performance,
He'd briefly say
Something like: *This is*

A marvelous song
From the mind of
Mr. Sam Pereira,
Arranged by
Nelson Riddle. Frank's

Dead now, of course,
Rolling craps
At the Sands Heaven.
His arm clutches
A large blonde, who

Might just be the woman
You are thinking
She is. He tells her
About what he did
Back home, alive

And over pasta with
The boys. He mentions
Cole Porter, and
Shakes his head; then
He, again, mentions you.

Hezekiah Allen Taylor

men who idolize Frank Sinatra

wear fedoras like Sammy mid-note
drink scotch like Dino, with a woman draped
seductively, loosely, like velvet cording

they hate to be called sir
as a doctor, they're called doc
they're highly unlikely to be a cardinal
or a rabbi or a baron

they live in apartments
not a mansion
nor a house
nor a shack

if all things are equal,
they'd rather not sing

and they wear tailored suits
no matter the theme
or humidity

you see, that's the hair shirt,
the itch for an art that you can't quite scratch;
you recognize it because it proves
you believe.

Francine DuBois

Men Who Idolize Frank Sinatra

Invest too much in hats, alcohol, and starlets,
But, on the bright side, they never get "Mr. Roboto"
Stuck in their dapper-hatted heads.

Jez Lowe

Had Away, Gan On

The sky was scarred with rainbows
And bruised black with April showers
It was warm at Sydney Harbour Bridge
But as wet as Blackpool Tower
And the man with the mandolin last night
Was weeping deep for Dublin
As I practiced basic native tongue
On the French girl I was cuddling

Chorus:
I said
Had away, gan on
Why man what ya deenin'
Well, I wish that I was back with them
That know just what I mean
When I say had away, gan on

The Yankee on the aeroplane said man you're white
        with terror
I said I much prefer the terra firma down there marra
He said you are a Scotsman
I said only when I'm angry
He smiled and said your humour tells me
You must be a Cockney

Chorus

That customs man in shorts and cream
Was as hairy as a carpet
He said mate, what's your football team I said
        Hartlepool United
He said me father saw them play once back in '67
When he to fake a gamy leg
When they couldn't make eleven.

Chorus

Last night a woman said
I had the style of Frank Sinatra
A professor up from Wollongong
Said I had the pen of Jean Paul Sartre
And a Scotsman said me songs were shite
And me accent was a scandal
And the only true born Geordies left were
Sting and Johnny Handle

Chorus

And if I'd learned the songs I should
I'd sing you "Blaydon Races"
But all I know are Dylan songs
And that single by Oasis
I dreamed I saw old Bob last night
He was drunker than a scuttle
He was trying to play some slide guitar with a Newcastle
        Brown Ale bottle

Chorus:
I said
Had away, gan on
Why man what ya deenin'
Well, I wish that I was back with them
That know just what I mean
When I say had away, gan on

Meg Kearney

Dreaming in Manhattan

Two bras, just washed, hang like bats from the showerhead;
a third one flies out the window and heads north on the FDR

Drive, leaving a trail of Woolite in its wireless wake. Traffic's
clogged like a bad heart. Horns hammer the air. "Bet that

flying bra tastes like the Yankees!" says a cabbie to a limo
driver idling in the next lane. "More like Marilyn Monroe,"

says the chauffeur. But now that C-cup's headed west, making
a bee-line for Hoboken, where pilgrims crawl the sidewalks

searching for Sinatra's humble abode. "They've gone blue-
eyed," the locals say, proof that Hobokeans don't know

where Sinatra was born, either. "God is in the potting shed,"
says the Scot tending bar at the Bloodaxe, "and that's all

ye need to know." Back in Manhattan, the burned bras of '64
rain like ash on the stock-broker's Volkswagen bus.

"My kingdom for a D-cup and a credit card!" shrieks
the flying bra to the fishergirls at Chelsea Piers. Just then,

Margie cycles up with her rod & reel and snatches that laundry
down. "From this day forward," says Margie, "a bra flying west

signals a drop in the divorce rate. Call it an omen with cleavage."
C'est la vie! sings the bra, headed back to its day job. Meanwhile,

behind the limo's tinted windows, Yogi and Marilyn clink
        glasses
and kiss, champagne spilling down their chins into paradise.

Bruce Taylor

The Year the Crooner Died

It was the year men stopped
shining their shoes, guys who had
the world on a string, it was the summer
the string broke.

Le Corbusier completes his Chapel
of *Notre Dame du Haut at Ronchamp*
while in 30,000 motels all across America
stunned flies die agonized dreamy
and demented on window sills.

And gals and dolls and chicks in
brassieres pale blue and bulletproof,
in exotic fur and zircon chokers swooned
to nothing else all night on the radio
as if they had ever much before.

The S.S. Andrea Doria goes down in heavy fog
60 miles off Nantucket. Jackson Pollack
is run down on Long Island.
Polish workers riot at Poznan.
Gas is 294 a gallon. Broadway went one way

There were a hundred words for guys
who were crooked, stupid, cheap.
Everybody knew a moke, a dope
or a punk as soon as he showed up
but there was only one word for him.

"Cool," of course, comes to mind,
not the smart ass way they say it today,
not flip and slickly ironic, but the way
everybody who knew what it meant
used to say it then, "Cool."

And not any of the dozen ways
We learned to say it later,
beat, broken, black-listed
and Buddha-ed out,
not even the way brothers

sassed, saxed and slapped it,
hopelessly hip, high and jive
or how some had to say it later,
hushed and out of harm's way,
a chill warning to be still,

or irreproducibly, in the 60s,
unless you're on acid at the time
and one C minus away from Vietnam,
all intake of breath and a giving out,
up off and over to everything,

but slow, and low, like slipping into
something silky brown and smokey,
like breathing in to breathe out,
like believing "Cool" was something
something could still get away with being.

The year they razed the 3rd Avenue El
the year coke became Coke
the year they introduced Crest and Special K
the year it was an all New York Series
and the Bums finally won.

Ulf Kirchdorfer

Asking Frank for Nancy

I confess
I have lusted
after
your daughter,
on a motorcycle,
the white
go-go boots,
and that song
in my ears,
the tough act
of boots
doing their thing,
like Plath,
only in a much more
wicked,
alive kind of way.

My first inclination
was to ask
your permission
to kiss
your daughter,
but I think
you, then Nancy,
would punch me
in the mouth
if I really
thought
Sinatra blood
flowed
passive,
I was standing
on some
Midwestern porch.

David Trinidad

Movin' with Nancy

It is almost time to grow up
I eat my TV dinner and watch
Nancy Sinatra in 1966
All boots and thick blonde hair

I eat my TV dinner and watch
The daughter of Frank Sinatra
All boots and thick blonde hair
She appears on "The Ed Sullivan Show"

The daughter of Frank Sinatra
She sings "These Boots Are Made For Walkin'"
She appears on "The Ed Sullivan Show"
The song becomes a number one hit

She sings "These Boots Are Made For Walkin'"
She sings "Somethin' Stupid" with her father
The song becomes a number one hit
She marries and divorces singer/actor Tommy Sands

She sings "Somethin' Stupid" with her father
She sings "The Last of The Secret Agents"
She marries and divorces singer/actor Tommy Sands
She sings "How Does That Grab You, Darlin'?"

She sings "The Last of the Secret Agents"
She sings "Lightning's Girl" and "Friday's Child"
She sings "How Does That Grab You, Darlin'?"
She sings "Love Eyes" and "Sugar Town"

She sings "Lightning's Girl" and "Friday's Child"
She puts herself in the hands of writer/producer Lee
    Hazelwood
She sings "Love Eyes" and "Sugar Town"
She co-stars with Elvis Presley in *Speedway*

She puts herself in the hands of writer/producer Lee
    Hazelwood
Three gold records later
She co-stars with Elvis Presley in *Speedway*
She rides on Peter Fonda's motorcycle

Three gold records later
She has developed an identity of her own
She rides on Peter Fonda's motorcycle
The wild angels roar into town

She has developed an identity of her own
Nancy Sinatra in 1966
The wild angels roar into town
It is almost time to grow up

Mary Ann Samyn

The Third Mirror Displacement

after Robert Smithson

Previously, several topics had existed:
Nancy Sinatra and beauty culture,
Emily Dickinson and solar wind.

But then the high school girl with bad teeth
interrupted.

Was this what Smithson called "sham
space," where I had been
inert, believing in "objects":

>   Sinatra's boots,
>   Dickinson in white on a high shelf...

Even a poem is just a thought
cast off, he'd say, false as an angel.

Positive or negative is no way to think,
especially if it's your job
to be the mirror.

Smithson, for example, went down a road
of butterflies and laid his mirrors
in crushed limestone.

Moments of flight mixed then
with moments of gravel as fleetingness took over.

This is how perception works.

(…Nancy and Emily understood)

if I knew more about it, I'd say
her skin was pale but flawless,

bits of cheekbone, like a swallowtail's wing,
fluttering in and out of focus…

David Lloyd

Reading Emily Dickinson

In Arthur and Marilyn's living room,
Frank's bored with his drink, his bowl of cashews,
the shouting from the kitchen.
It's going to be a long night.

He glances around, checks out a painting
that he never understood,
scans the books under the coffee table,
picks one up, opens it:

"Tell all the Truth but tell it slant – Success..."
Then, "My Life had stood – a Loaded Gun – "
And then, "Vesuvius – at Home."

More shouts from the kitchen. A glass breaks.

Not bad, he thinks, and continues:
"Zero at the Bone" and
"I heard a Fly buzz when I died"
just as Marilyn pops her head – then herself –
around the door,

mascara smudged, martini swirling,
its olive a world dislodged from orbit.
Her lips await the next kiss.

Who cares? Frank thinks, shutting the book.
Not me.

Arthur's a no-show, sitting at the kitchen table,
his face firmly in his hands.

Matt Santateresa

Frank Sinatra, Drunk, Turns His Gunsights on a Dolphin off Corsica

1.

Being without a certain lady is unfortunate, luckless,
you could say
and Hemingway sounds serious, noting in his moleskin
a member of parliament being embraced by an
attractive woman, slightly wet
in the arena crowd this sweltering day, as Frank, off the
isle
of Corsica, where Napoleon was born, with impolite
noises, and his yacht
coursing through teal waves down from Genoa where
Doges preyed
as if sub-pharaohs, their spirits jailed in dung beetle
carapaces swung
underworld, they sit in fringed clothes immune as
Napoleon, as Frank
observes the dolphins like silver archdukes leap out of
the surface, it is noon
on the Mediterranean, the dolphins run parallel to the
speeding boat
Frank is in an anarchistic drunken state above laws
curlicues and serif and
ridiculous heavy handed bunk, he exhorts, 'attaboy' as
he lines one up, the motor
drones like a sermon, his 40-40, eye squint, a fluorescent
gleam of its religious skin
to get closer he leans over the stainless steel railing,
hard against his groin
and tries to end the short pilgrimage, squeezes the
trigger, thinking
of Joey Bishop's line about Las Vegas, laughs and misses,
the dolphin
slips back maturely, but not before spotting Frank

laughing in his teal tee
shirt, the one with the white palms, the bullet spins
through water leaving a
small boiling wake.
The dolphin stays under and sees Napoleon, then
dodges
and winks in its sinusoidal movements, like a libretto
from a consummate altruist –
the second bullet that jams in the feed infuriates Frank.

2.

The bullring crowd rises to its feet, the matador sings in
pain
as a bright tip of horn scalpels through his costume
broach and tidbits of baubles, breaks the skin, enters
subcutaneous and deeper
as sweat and blood snorts into aerosol spume and
momentarily takes the shape of a rose.

Lawrence Upton

Sinatra

Just knowing you don't have to be kind
to sing true; appearing both good and bad;
often sharp, much as a broken bottle is,
sometimes holding himself checked; Sinatra sang.

You don't need to have a good voice to sound
more than good. It's what you do with the song,
how it's arranged. And he used arrangers,
the best, even if they started O.K.

but no more. It was time-based; that time's passed.
And the man was so popularly influential
that, retrospectively, even what's dull's
heard brightly: rubbery things; monstrosities;

which ant imaginations now stretch out
over what is worthy, as it once was.

Landis Everson

Our Boy, Sinatra

He had a tendency toward ego
that improved with age,
to possess everything he could swallow
and pawn it off in song.

He made everything belong
to him — a generation so innocent
it was hypnotized
by his hands
strangling microphones, strung out

on the slavish two-step,
the rhythm
of his age. I have heard he was armed
and dangerous only to those
who opened their eyes

around his ownership
of the soft
and mawkishly inclined,
not charmed
dumb enough by stars,
America and Vegas dust,

to just shuffle on like us and
sway and swoon
behind the strut and croon
of Mister
Frank Sinatra's I'm-one-of-youse-guys,
dreamy,
ripped-off tunes.

Greg Rappleye

From the Vegas Cantos

"Hey, I like to swing as much as anybody,
but this ain't a plan, it's a pipe load of the
crazy stuff."
    Dean Martin, from the original shooting
    script for Ocean's Eleven.

January 1960. Kleig lights, Sinatra
at the Sands, filming underway
for the Rat Pack movie, the Strip
blazing neon. The plot, such as it is:
Eleven ex-soldiers, led by Frank,
Rob five casinos on New Year's Eve,
after Sammy knocks out the power lines.
Every day, the production shoots into dusk.
Cesar Romero as Duke Santos,
trying to intimidate the boys,
Sammy driving the truck full of money
through the Sheriff's blockade,
Angie Dickinson telling Ilka Chase
just how it is between Angie and Frank,
how it's always going to be, five different bands
playing *Auld Lang Syne,* over and over,
dancing into the New Frontier.
It's hard work and at night they unwind
with vodka martinis, a bottle
of Jack Daniels, a splash of soda,
unfiltered Chesterfields. *Smoking is all*
in the wrist, Lawford says.

At one a.m.,
Frank backs away from the piano
in the Copa Room, says, *The action here*
is getting old, to Sammy, Sammy nods at Dean,
the Pack rises, pushes toward the exit.

In the parking lot, three El Dorado
convertibles: One pearlescent blue,
one lemon chiffon, one green mist,
all courtesy of Jack Warner.
They load the cars, tops down.
It's January in the desert, but a warm front
has burgeoned up from the Sea of Cortez,
and Dean says, *It's ragtop weather baby*,
nudging the strapless breasts
of a showgirl's sequined gown.
Frank and Dean in front, Angie, Ilka,
then Sammy driving the chiffon El Dorado,
Lawford sipping a traveler, more girls,
Joey Bishop, the only sober one,
driving the third car, *worried*, Romero,
drunk and laughing, Shirley MacLaine
and another chick in back. *Does Frank know
where's he going?* Joey wants to know.
It's your job to be the mother! Romero says.
And too often Joey thinks *Right*, I'm the one
left paying for broken windows
and slipping fifty to the maitre d'
while the others scoot through the kitchen,
playing pat-ass on the way. Behind
the third Cadillac, the parking attendant,
Paco, drives his '53 Chevy pickup—
Richard Conte, already swan-songed
in the movie (*Your guy buys the big casino*,
Frank had explained), flat-drunk
in the bed of the truck, Henry Silva,
Norman Fell, and a couple of broads
holding stakes that rise from the sides,
everyone singing *Come Fly with Me*,
Frank's number one hit.

On they go,
Ten twenty miles into the desert,
until Romero begins to wonder if this is
such a good idea, until the singing stops
and the girls have started to shiver.
Dean lights another cigarette, looks
sideways at Frank, who has said almost nothing.
Just as Dean is about to ask, *What's up, amigo?*
Frank goes, *This is the place*, jerks the car
onto a two-track, bottoms through the alkalai flats
and drives on. Sammy, his good eye almost hypnotized
by the dashing lines of U.S. 95,
comes to, chases the pearlescent blue
El Dorado off the road,
the green Cadillac and flat-grey pickup
follow suit. Frank finally stops, hops
out, his car in park, headlights
still on. *Circle up!* He yells, looping a finger
in the air. Frank backs the drivers off,
making sure they leave enough space
in the middle. Everyone piles out.
Paco! Frank snaps. *You and Normie*
grab some branches off that pile of mesquite!
Dean, Sammy, get the booze and blankets
outta the trunk. You girls, there's a cooler
and snacks in the yellow El Dorado.
And while you're up, Dean,
Tune all the radios to that Mexican station
we've been listening to!
Sammy squirts the mesquite
with lighter fluid, tosses a match,
the oily flames rise into the sky,
the radios begin three hours of Basie,
Ellington, and Dorsey, between songs
the announcer hawking headache powders,
Geritola and *laxantes*.

A chill in the air. Stars swirl overhead,
miles from the neon clutter of the Strip.
Some pair off under blankets.
Sammy has a few drinks, smokes,
takes a chick he's been eyeing
into the lemon El Dorado. Her head
disappears, Sammy lies back against the creamy leather.
You are the craziest, he says over and over.
Dean chases Shirley around the fire.
She lets him catch up, paw her, stick his tongue
down her throat, bending her
in the crook of his left arm, martini balanced
in one hand, cigarette in the other.
Baby, he says, *let's rehearse our scene*.
She laughs, pushes him away, the pursuit begins
again.

Night goes by. Constellations rise.
Paco tends the fire. Romero falls asleep,
Norman Fell nods off, Silva wanders away,
Sammy snores in the El Dorado,
The sweet head of a showgirl in his lap,
How are Things in Glocca Morra?
Take the "A" Train,
Ac-cent-tchu-ate the Positive,
50,000 watts of Ensenada clear-channel
play on. Only Frank, Angie,
and Joey stay awake, Frank listening
to music, pacing, singing a scrap lyric,
cupping a cigarette to his face,
pushing a black panama snap-brim
back on his head, occasionally lighting
a Chesterfield for Angie. A sweet smell is
in the air, a redolence Frank knows
from the early forties—
the bad boys in the saxophone section.
Frank looks toward the pickup.
He sees the glow: Paco, Dean, and Lawford
passing a pipe of Mary Jane,

wacky tabacky, the crazy stuff.
Frank frowns. *They're in the desert, okay,*
no one around and if you stay clear
of the Mormons, anything goes,
but he doesn't need any hopheads
hanging around, capisce?
He looks at Angie, nods toward
the pickup, she shakes her head
in disapproval. *Take care of it*, Frank snaps
at Joey, then turns and walks
to the other side of the fire.

Stars turn. The fire burns down.
Frank looks at his watch. Almost 6 a.m.
He tells Joey, *Radios off. And roust Dean*
outta the truck, he's got to see this.
Frank steps fifty yards into the desert.
A few minutes later, Joey and Angie follow.
Dean, his head pounding, stumbles toward them.
Suddenly, the horizon ignites—soundless,
a half-moon of orange, yellow, and white fire
swells in the distance. Frank's face flashes
in the ignited air, he squints, heads jerk
back in alarm, a reaction to light,
Oh my God, Angie mouths, and Joey and Dean
just stand there. The blankets stir.
Sammy's head wobbles,
his good eye opens, a sleepy head
rises from his lap. Paco moans to consciousness,
begins to cross himself,
and before he gets to *Espiritu Santo*,
a windstorm sweeps through—just
dust glows red below
the expanding mushroom cloud,
a concussion washes their bodies,
the earth begins to roll,
everyone is awake now—even Conte's head rises
behind the pickup cab.
To the east, the air is on fire, electric

With the bomb's ignition,
That's what I brought you to see,
Frank says, *the Big Kahplowie!*
Raising a glass of bourbon
Toward the towering firestorm,
Salud to Armageddon! He yells into the dust, turns
And tells everyone, *Pack it in*
Before the fallout hits! He throws the keys of the blue
      El Dorado at Dean.
You're sober. Drive. Joey,
Take the yellow one. Lawford, the green.
Paco drives his own. Angie, you ride with me.
The caravan sets out. Conte stirs again,
Silva wipes atomic dust from his eyes.

In the back of the blue El Dorado,
Sinatra curls into the fetal position, his head
nested in Angie's lap. She smooths his cheek,
his face softens in the courtesy lights.
The radio is off, Dean in front, smoking
and driving, the horizon beginning to glow
with the orange and streaky pink
of a bombed-out desert sunrise. Ahead,
the other glow of the Strip. Dean
finishes a cigarette, looks at it for a second
then flicks it over the side. In the mirror,
he watches it bounce and spray sparks
across the road, until it disappears
in the headlight-wash of the lemon El Dorado.
He begins to sing his new song
from the movie, scatting it, arriving
at the chorus, tapping his fingers on the wheel.
Ain't that a kick in the head?
he sings, A*in't that a kick in the head?*

David Lloyd

The Heavens

All the moths of Nevada seek out
these infamous lights, immolating themselves
in countless sparks on the "S" and the "d"
of the Sands Hotel.

With all the shuffling, rolling, clanking
money machines, the infinite décolletage
and spinning ice cubes, the smoke
and the mirrors, no one sees
this dusty descent of bodies and wings,
antennae and legs, the steady yearning,
the tiny deaths that don't stop.

No one sees, that is, but Frank,
staring up from the balcony of his three-bedroom,
second-floor suite, cigarette poised between fingers,
a Jack Daniels on the rocks with a twist
and a swizzle at the ready.
Where do they come from? He asks,
as if a flunky with an answer was waiting.
Why, he wants to know, *don't they stop?*

Frank leans further out and squints.
But no stars dot this desert sky. No meteors
beginning somewhere, ending elsewhere.
No revelations beyond what revolving numbers can tell.
Here, the earth casts its brilliant shadow
over all the heavens, everywhere and forever.

Frank shrugs his shoulders,
checks his watch, tightens the knot
of his tie, flicks a half-inch of ash
over the railing for the desert breeze to dissect.
Downstairs the Copa waits.

Allen Ginsberg

Las Vegas: Verses Improvised for
El Dorado H.S. Newspaper

Aztec sandstone waterholes known by Moapa've
dried out under the baccarat pits
of M.G.M.'s Grand Hotel.

If Robert Maheu knew
                who killed Kennedy
would he tell Santos Trafficante?

If Frank Sinatra had to grow his own
                food, would he learn
how to grind piñon nuts?

If Sammy Davis had to find original water
would he lead a million old ladies laughing
        round Mt. Charleston to the Sheephead Mountains
                in migratory cycle?

Does Englebert know the name of
the mountains he sings in?

When gas and water dry up
will wild mustangs
        inhabit the Hilton Arcade?

Will the 130-billion-dollared-Pentagon guard
        the radioactive waste dump at Beatty
                for the whole Platonic Year?

Tell all the generals and Maitre D's
to read the bronze inscriptions
        under the astronomical flagpole at Hoover Dam.

Will Franklin Delano Roosevelt
        Bugsy Siegel and Buddha
all lose their shirts at Las Vegas?

Yeah! Because they don't know how to gamble
        like mustangs and desert lizards.

William Hathaway

Why That's Bob Hope

The comedian, holding a chunk of flaming shale.
If only *Der Bingle* could see him now! He looked
so puffed and sleepy in that Texaco hardhat,
I could've popped a fuse. Well, like the oil,
here today and gone today. In *my* good old days
Hope was on Sullivan's "shew" so often us kids
dropped TV for longhair sex and smoking weeds.
What a mistake! But now we're past our wild phase
and Bob's back with this burning rock, funny
for a change. No, no old quips about Dean's double
vision, Phyllis Diller's sagging breasts or Sinatra's aging
          treble.
He says if we all squeeze the rock together real money
will drip out. We'll live real good and still afford a war
where he'll bust our boys' guts on tour in El Salvador.

Al Jolson
(Asa Yoelson)

If you never heard of me,
You ain't heard nuthin' yet!
The World's Greatest Entertainer!
That's what they called me.
And they were right.
When I was a little kid
I ran away from home
In Washington, D.C.,
To be a drummer boy
In the Spanish-American War.
That's a long time ago!
But I can talk about it now,
'Cause nobody can kid me
About having a young wife any more!
After I got out of the Army,
(They threw me out, 'cause I was
Awful young!)
I went to California.
I did a little boxin',
And I was real good, too!
But I wanted to sing
I come by it naturally,
For my father sometimes took
The cantor's place
In the synagogue
In the little town in Russia,
Where I was born.
I actually started
My career as an entertainer
In nineteen hundred and six,
Around the time of the big fire
In San Francisco.
And from then on, *boom*!

Star of a minstrel show!
Vaudeville headliner!
Then, the Winter Garden in New York!
And then, for a zillion years,
The World's Greatest Entertainer!
And listen!
You ain't heard nuthin' yet!
When I was way past sixty
I was still making movies.
And when I wasn't in 'em in person,
They made my voice come out
Of an unknown kid's mouth!
And every one of 'em
Was a big success!
My records sold by the millions!
And I beat the stock market,
And I won at the race track!
Whatever I did,
I bowled everybody over!
The story they told
In the movie of my life
Was truer than the other life stories
They've made since.
They showed me
As a man who was only happy
When he was singin'
Or bowin' to great applause.
I never cared much
About anything
Or anybody....
I grew away from my family.
I had very few friends
Among the actors.
I didn't want to hear 'em talk
About what a hit they made
In some small town.
That was nuthin' to what I did!
I stood 'em in the aisles
Wherever I went.

Brother, I was *somethin'*!
Nothing bothers me much now,
Except, maybe
I should've been kinder
To the fellow who was with me
For nearly forty years.
His name was Louis Epstein.
"Eppie," I used to call him.
I intended to do
A lot for him
And for my piano player,
Harry Akst.
But I never got around
To puttin' it on paper.
I didn't know
I was going to die so quick!
I was gettin' ready
To do a show with Bing,
And *boom!* I was here.
I guess the best I can say now
Is that I'm a little sorry.
Sometimes I wish
I could come back
On a vaudeville show,
With Sinatra, and Como,
And Sands, and Elvis,
And yes, little ol' Bing!
I would like to go on last,
Like I always did,
And throw the microphone
Off the stage.
Who needed it?
I sang at Yankee Stadium
Without it.
I followed Caruso,
Singin' "Over There"!
After he'd sung it!
I followed him right on
At the Century Theatre,

And I said:
Folks, you ain't heard nuthin' yet!
These kids that are singin' today,
They make me laugh…
If you want to really hear 'em
You gotta hug 'em.
Sometimes I wish
I had a real son,
My own flesh and blood.
Then I could've watched him
Take up where I left off.
But come to think of it
I woulda' been disappointed.
He couldn't have been
As good as I was!
Nobody was!
And you wanna know somethin'?
Nobody is!

Emily XYZ

Sinatra walks out
(voice A)

The bars close and Sinatra walks out,
just a man in a hat and a trench coat
A standing ovation always follows

He is a terminal delinquent
in a bad mood
a temper tantrum over three generations
age has not mellowed nor time sweetened him –
He is the greatest of them all

He is the last man I want to
applaud
The opposite of Andy Warhol
is Frank Sinatra
Irredeemably corny
violent heavy-handed and horny
he is all / he is nothing at all
You cannot makes jokes
about Frank Sinatra

don't even know they have
moved me to tears
night I met my first wife
Some say he speaks for men
men unable to speak
unfortunate men of the 20th Century
trapped in ridiculous cages
cages they never imagined
cages of their own making

(voice B)

because he is such an incredible
entertainer,
an inspiration to three generations

He is the greatest of them all
He is the living embodiment of the fine
tradition of macho
American
overkill—

sleep with
The opposite of Andy Warhol
is Frank Sinatra

You cannot make jokes
about Frank Sinatra
Some say he sings like a dream
and gives voices to emotions most men
can never admit to
that tie up the heart
or break it to pieces
Some say he speaks for men
men unable to speak
unfortunate men of the 20th century
trapped in ridiculous cages
cages they never imagined
cages of their own making

In the 50s, his cloven hooves
marked up many a bandstand – Critics said
QUIT!
Hit it!

Sicilian
Sicilian
Sicilian
Sicilian
Jilly Rizzo –

blood/ blood alcohol content
blood brotherhood
WNEW AM 11-3-0
Nelson Riddle
Axel Stordahl
Earl Wilson
Jule Styne
Sammy Cahn
Sammy Davis Jr
Toots Shor –
He likes it when people call him a
class act
it confirms his own opinion
If he is misunderstood
it is because he is confusing –
This fabulous gift,
Stored in the case of such a troubled man
Sad!
Got a telegram from Sinatra
Here's what it said:

Some say he belongs in prison,
him and his mob connections
You know what they say
but nothing was proven—
In the 50, his cloven hooves
marked up many a bandstand—Critics said
QUIT!

Who does he think he is?
Overly sensitive
Split personality
Schizy,
scary
Jilly Rizzo—
alcohol / alcohol
alcohol content / alcohol content
rat pack
Radio City Music Hall
Jimmy van Heusen
Johnny Mercer
Harold Arlen
William B. Williams
Sam Giancana
Cole Porter
Toots Shor—

class act

If he is misunderstood
it is because he's an asshole—
Your fabulous face always
grimacing at reporters—
Don't make me laugh!

YOUR INFORMATION STINKS,
LADY
Broads always think they know best,

Right!
Don't talk to me baby you're
not in my league, not in my league,
Where'd you where'd you
Where'd you wear you wear
The way you wear your hat
the way you sip your tea
the memory of all that
oh no they can't
take that away from me
the way your smile just beams
The way you sing off key
the way you haunt my dreams

In a dream, Sinatra is awakened by 20-year-old
Mia Farrow as the ghost of his own past

She comes in the night
praising his phrasing
His voice clear of vibrato
natural as conversation
melodious and cool is restored.
She shows him Pearl Jam
She shows him Pantera
and he slams them
and when he slams them, everybody says
WELL, FRANK'S RIGHT!
ROCK N ROLL DOES SUCK
Somehow the past feels like
a better place / A place where Ava
Gardner bakes coconut cakes
a place without Elvis
a world of his own
where all men are equal brutal
insufferable laughable
childish homophobe RICH

Right!
Don't talk to me baby you're
not in my league, not in my league,
Where'd you get that information
you're a leech, man, you're a
parasite, just like the rest of them
get it? Cunt, C-U-N-T
you know what that who what is don't
you been layin' down for that two
dollars all your life that stench you
that stench you smell is coming from her!
I don't want to talk to you go home
you go home and take a bath
let's get the hell outta here baby you're
nothing but a TRAMP TRAMP TRAMP

*Strangers in the night
exchanging glances
wondering in the night
what were the chances
we'd be sharing love
before the night was through*

WELL, FRANK'S RIGHT!
ROCK N ROLL DOES SUCK

a better place / A place where Ava
Gardner bakes coconut cakes
a place without Elvis
a world of his own
where he is the leader
postwar Las Vegas mafia royalty
Hollywood underworld RICH
The 60s the rest of us remember
are as a little museum to Frank Sinatra

a small curious place
where Viet Nam and Watts

and there's a box
containing Pink Floyd
Eldridge Cleaver Bernadette Devlin
everything Mark Rudd ever said

Those he understands!
Back from engagements beyond the grave,
old friends visit Sinatra backstage
Sammy Davis Jr. falls on him weeping,
tells him
Baby / You're the Chairman of the Board!
Joe E. Lewis is glad to be back
He says Vegas is better than heaven
Deeper cleavage and lost more booze
Opens a bottle / Here's to the boys –
They don't notice / the club is closing
They don't notice the passing of time
because they're drunk
because they're has-beens
because they're famous
because they're boys –

The real problem is mortality
The real problem is nothing lasts
Gotta grow up sometime / Life is short
songs finish
God plays dice
in this casino right here
The real problem is
body and soul don't mix

a small curious place
where Viet Nam and Watts play
constantly in a silent loop
on the video monitor,
and there's a box
containing the Stones, Hendrix
Dennis Hopper Malcolm McDowell
and the whole Stax Volt catalogue
all incomprehensible to Frank
Only thing in the whole decade
Makes any sense to him is Mrs. Robinson's
stockinged legs —
Those he understands!

Baby / You're the Chairman of the Board!

He says Vegas is better than heaven

They don't notice / the club is closing
They don't notice the passing of time
because their wives
because their hormones
because their fans
because they're drunk —
but you know somethin'
way I see it
the real problem is mortality
The real problem is you get old and die
Gotta go sometime / Time is short
beauty vanishes
God knows why
this world's the way it is
The real problem is
life doesn't make sense —
WHY DON'T YOU JUST

The boundaries of good taste and human
decency having been crossed and crossed out
again and again by the bourbon in his
glass,
Frank Sinatra stands and offers a toast:

To the human race
To hell with the human race!
Nancy with the laughing face,
what has she ever done for me!
All you mothers are worthless –
There's nobody in my league!

Mr. Sinatra
how can anyone so wretched
sing so well?

(*In unison*)
A person is only a case
A holder for all manner of things
A random arrangement of idiocy and glory
Sometimes a barrage of artistic light
Sometimes an embarrassment,
a dismaying puddle of slush
Sometimes a nobody,
fading into a crowd or the distance

SHUT UP AND SING

bloodstream

To the human race

To hell with the human race!
Bunch of buck and half hookers,
what have they ever done for me!
All you mothers are worthless—
There's nobody in my league!

Placing myself on his good side I raise
my hand to ask a question:
Mr. Sinatra,
how can anyone so wretched
sing so well?
I'm not the first
and I won't be the last
one born
a walking contradiction,
dead on from the heart
the rest all thrown together,
hitting the same walls
over
and over
and over—

(*In unison*)
A person is only a case
A holder for all manner of things
A random arrangement of idiocy and glory
Sometimes a barrage of artistic light
Sometimes an embarrassment,
a dismaying puddle of slush
Sometimes a nobody,
fading into a crowd or the distance

the welfare office
the supermarket
the laundromat, the library
and sometimes
marvelous as a god,
all in one
all in one lifetime
all in one life.

Doo be doo be doo, doo doo doo do do

the welfare office
the supermarket
the laundromat, the library
and sometimes
marvelous as a god,
all in one
all in one lifetime
all in one life.

Doo be doo be doo, doo doo doo do do

Reuben Jackson

Frank

like god
or miles,
no second name is
needed.

as opposed to
"reservation for sinatra;
party of 37.

can I get a last name
for the maitre'd
you understand."

the heart needs
no such pretense

when "in the wee small hours"
plays,

its longing
unpretentious
and haunting as
moonlight.

a 32 bar ashram;

peace from a boy
from Hoboken

if he was an asskicker,
so be it.

I think of the brilliant brown voices
of my youth;

they too needed
protection,

and nights when
the angels needed
rest.

I dared not replace his
albums

in stores where my face is
familiar

because my love for his sound
is as personal as
stretchmarks

surrounding my ribcage
like rings on a tree
old enough to remember

"all the things you
are."

Robert Sheppard

Angel at the Junk Box

im Frank Sinatra
Midnight Ride 3
IM 7
Twentieth Century Blues 57

I.

Breath betweens the sexy brass
quakes against the battlements of the tier;

lute song off the blames. Moaning mini-
symphonics underwrite maze blazing of cries
in the mids of my faces...

-dict no dirty crowd, taut; taughts,
held and slackened to twirl, waver-

songing

II.

Cooling, she might hear you
sing and *know* the same words
and shift.
         Cash it now and every blip
is a dizzy how. Propelled
into a cringe, wrapped
in a growl:

the way you mock your blands

III.
Mute up your factitious sensation
(even a ring of breath to kill)
Transmute a crazed phrase of male hysterics
Break up this song into this gut-voiced holding

IV.
Bounce a pebble voice on the
waves of this smile could then
if the sinking full-bowled
potential point of inform

Poison emotion. Floors crawl
a new song, doesn't fluff? A
strange stress on not-speech.
Hats on your horns gentlemen!

Ease a sample hammer
on the fall, blast over the stock.
Repeats; repeat tobacco-toned town;
the voice in my shivering circle.

V.
Black Kansas, sit! Sudden guitar
gets it odderly

Hear those folded arms and clarity —
the doors of deception off-beats up-beat a
croak to the full;

risking flats affirm music

space him still low

spread to the lowest in time
to the admissible

last syllable cymbal out(→)s

Lenny Lianne

The Worst Lamb

I'll begin by saying April stinks
Belladonna, lilacs
        and hyacinths.

All-ee, all-ee, in free:
The pub's a-closin'.
Sturm und drang, ach, verboten.

Rama lama Kama Sutra.
My way, my way, Frank Sinatra.

Who cares if Mr. Kurtz he dead?
Dharma, dharma,
        Dharma and Greg.

Maria Mazziotti Gillan

I Am Here in the Pathmark Among the Cheeses

I am here in the Pathmark among the cheeses
when I remember learning how to dance, my older
sister, playing the man, leading me around the dining
room in the 19th street apartment, one/two/three/four,
one/two/three/four. The music, violins and horns,
Frank Sinatra singing, my body stiff and awkward,
my sister pushing, tugging, trying to teach me
a rhythm that was born in her bones. *Loosen up*,
she kept saying, *loosen up*, and I tried but my body
refused to be anything but shy and terrified. My sister
always loved to dance, with her Marilyn Monroe body,
her slender, perfectly formed legs and feet, her high
heels, her full, sexy lips painted with *Fire and Ice*
her straight teeth.

I am here in the Pathmark, staring at the refrigerator
case with its hunks of provolone and mozzarella,
cheddar and longhorn, assaulted by the memory
of the nights we sat together at my sister's house
eating cheese and crackers and drinking highballs
and talking, how those nights gradually thinned out
and finally disappeared after my sister, diagnosed
at thirty with rheumatoid arthritis, got gradually worse
and worse, until by forty-five, when her hands
and feet were so obviously deformed, she stopped
wanting to be social, though she'd always been
gregarious and outgoing.

Finally she could no longer dance, her feet so twisted
the bones poked through the skin. I would sit in her
den, holding her hand, think of us as young girls,
my sister with her raging energy, her electric smile,
teaching me how to dance, her girlfriends
coming to the apartment where they danced

the jitterbug and rhumba while I watched, my sister
always happy to be moving, her body sexy and alive
in that room where we'd push the table out of the way
to make room so we could dance.

I see us clearly in the Pathmark's fluorescent lights,
and here, in the aisle next to the cheeses, I wish
I could talk to my sister again, my sister who is
already three years dead, wish that I still believed
in a heaven where my sister could be young again
and could spend her nights dancing
to Sinatra's maple-syrup voice.

SuGar

Robot Sings
(As If He Were Frank Sinatra with a Half-Boiled Egg and the Salt Shaker on a Breakfast Table)

My dear love
Tell me why your heart is so empty
Won't you dear
Deny your love for me is just whimsy

My mind is puzzled
While bacon in a pan is frizzled
Since you're so beautiful

You are my morning delight
I wake up to kiss you
I often spend a sleepless night
Just afraid of losing you

My hope has fizzled
The nightfall makes my heart drizzled
Love is so painful

Dana Gerringer and Kara L. C. Jones

Creation @ Dutch Treats

I sat in the window
and looked upon

unsheathed again
scabbard of skin
wondering why I
could never be yielded by him

and Sinatra played, making me weigh
the importance of life and love and hurt

one handle by the bathtub
one handle behind my ribs
I rode the tears up the steepest hill
and listened to the spokes catching on every breath

walking past the marquee, I thought it said Matrix
but really it said Marlene Dietrich & somehow
I tossed back in time, but

I only know the time by the traffic
the ones that time did not change for
nothing is ever so precious, as the moment
right before it brakes…

at the post office, the grumpy old man was mean but
outside the old man on the bench with the ice cream cone
was nice, and

the flowers on my plate were real
but I could not eat them
it seemed that nothing beautiful
would ever pass through me again…

and then,
in very un-original fashion,
we lived happily ever after.

Ruth Moon Kempher

Dinner, at *La Casa Amarilla*

The yellow house, I'm wondering
is *soltera* always "widow," or more as it sounds
"woman alone"? One candle gutters
doing its dance to Sinatra's scratchy clown song
and Alfonsina Storni open on the table, *Obra
Poetica* and two dogs hunkered down, patient
waiting for a string of chicken – noses up at squash
and cole slaw from a box.
                    The rhythms are close –
"*Primavera*" (comes from "first green")
and the lyric he sings, "Send in the clowns…"
The old hound dog Koko, now gone
                              she'd never sit still
chicken on the table, she'd hiphunch around
groaning. But these young pups sit
like straight-A students
                    with candle-flames for eyes.

        For tonight, I must
consider paragraph construction – *soltera* –
tomorrow's lesson – (with the lyric's moan, the cheap
cole slaw and broiled chicken and Frank's gone –
he turned older, *por Dios*, like the rest of us –
the recording sings his song with edges
like the rasp of time.) I'm distracted.
Low carbohydrates *muy poetica*, O very.

        Years back, I'd have sworn
it would be different. No squash, ever.
Swore that, to our Mrs. Rogers, the *soltera*
slop-heeled in my grandmother's kitchen

or was that cabbage? "When I grow up…"
Say it again now, chewing carefully
    "…No more squash." Dining
a la casa amarilla, my yellow house
that tilts itself sedately
into the swamp.

Joel Lewis

The September of My Years

I see a portrait hanging
of Frank Sinatra & the owner
of Veniero's, here in the East Village.
Sinatra is smiling as he holds up
the biggest cannoli made
since the Resurrection.

When was that photo taken, I ask
the waitress. "Those guys are both
dead," she says. I press further,
explain myself. She responds:
"I've only been here three months
& those guys were dead
when I got here!"

Sipping the dredges of a double espresso,
I daydream of a world that lacks sanctions.

Giovanna (Janet) Capone

I Met Her in Front of the Tomato Sauce

Aisle 5
at Lucky's, the low price leader.
She didn't know what brand to pick.
"Key buy!" She waved her hands. "They all say key buy."
"Get the Classico," I said pointing. "It's the best.
Either that, or Frank Sinatra. But they don't carry
            Frank Sinatra."
I pictured Frank Sinatra in someone's arms,
his wrinkled old face, gray hair, and banana nose.
I pointed at the Classico.
"Tomato and basil," I said.
Proud that I knew my bottled sauces.
"It's much better than Ragu."
But I hate this stuff in a jar!" she said,
turning my pride to shame.
I'm only Italian in name, I thought.
It's my worst fear. What if it's true?
"I'd rather make my own," she said, "but I'm too exhausted."
An Italian, I thought. A real one.
She had brown eyes and soft, bleached hair on her upper lip
And I remembered how
I used to bleach my own, many years ago.
That stuff stings like hell.
I can still remember the smell.
"Are you Italian?" I said.
"Oh, yes. I come from the old ways, where you cook
all day long and the whole house smells of sauce.
That's what my mother did. And it tastes so much better.
Not like this stuff in a jar! Do you ever make sauce like that?"
"Oh yeah," I said. "In fact, my mother makes great sauce too.
I learned it from her, but I don't have the time
these days."
I put a bottle
In my basket, feel sad, assimilated, and angry.

She's not the first Italian I've met
In the tomato sauce aisle
At the supermarket.
One day I followed
An old man and woman
Through the store.
I hardly ever get to hear Italian spoken
Anymore.
So I followed them, listening.
They looked like Aunt Tessie and Uncle Mike.

We should get a support group, I thought,
Italians in Transition
Grief support group for the descendents of immigrants,
Italy bleeding out of us with every passing year.
They want to bleach us white, leave us bloodless
and culturally flat.
Fuck that.
I wrote the ad in my head
Support group now forming
to explore issues of sauce and loss,
assimilation, annihilation and rage.
We could get up a support group, I thought,
as the woman in front of me talked a few more minutes
about language and dialect,
and how her parents never taught her Italian.
"Neither did mine," I said. "They only spoke it to each
          other. Neapolitan.
But I'm studying it now, in school," I added, with a
          mixture of frustration
and pride. From a young age, we're encouraged to hide
our Italian ways.
The whole person is not allowed
to develop
They pushed us to be American instead.
"I'm studying the language, but it's Florentine," I said,
"so it's not the same,"

and it brings up all my shame
Why don't I know how to speak Neapolitan?
Why didn't they teach me?
I'm 35
and here I am
in aisle 5
buying bottled sauce
at $2.65 a jar
Lucky's, the low price leader.
What is the cost, I thought,
of forced assimilation, the forced migration
of millions of people to a foreign land?
And can I really sell out, to such a low bid?

"Well, good for you!" she said, "for learning the language,
          I mean.
It is our mother tongue."
We parted ways
She headed for the bread,
and me for the frozen foods.
A bag of stuffed shells
and some Armanino's homemade ravioli
to go with the sauce.
Some grated parmesan
and a jar of Progresso sweet peppers
as some twelve stepper slogan
passed through my head.
"Came to believe a power greater than ourselves
could restore us to sanity."
Shit, I've been in California too long!
But what's wrong with a support group?
We could exchange recipes for sauce
figure out how to cope with loss
reinvent community
understand our ancestry
We could find our way back
to our culture.
Support group my ass! Some other voice said
We need a fucking political movement.

Move back to New York.
You're too damn soft! You're overcooked spaghetti
limp and disintegrating in the melting pot
you're shot!

At the check out stand
I ran into her again.
"Where did you say you're studying Italian?"
"At the community college," I said
as she put down her loaf of Italian bread.
I felt so fed
by that one question.
Twenty minutes later
she was still thinking about what we both said
thinking while shopping
the same thoughts running through our heads
about culture and tradition,
language,
and resisting
assimilation.

An hour later
in my kitchen
I remembered her dark brown eyes
The Italians I've met
on aisle 5
Ethnic pride
at Lucky's, the low price leader.

Gerry LaFemina

Portrait of My Father Playing Cards, Brooklyn 1975

See my father with a fan of five playing cards
 in his right hand, cigarette held in a tin ashtray
beside him. Blue smoke blurring our vision;

he thinks he looks like Sinatra in those Rat Pack Vegas
 films which is my father's vanity showing itself &
which we'll have to forgive because he's young as we watch –

perhaps only my age now – & because he's settled to believe
 the lies of old men who sit around tables & trust
in the beauty of chance: red & black suits; the blue

diamond-back pattern of the cards; the grimy hues of clay
 chips. Their towers before him expand & decrease
at intervals. I now understand what he prayed for then –

some success measurable by stakes & winning;
 what my mother prayed for: just that he'd come home.
What I prayed for: the sweet pomegranate I saw in the market.

How I loved its little jeweled seeds, each with a place
 in the fruit's husk. I watched him play cards like I
watched him take the razor to his chin & cheeks

each morning. Little cuts of blood on his neck, reminiscent
 of pomegranate staining my lips & tongue red,
not bloody as the faces of soldiers I saw on the news,

Huey Choppers stirring up a cumulonimbus of dust.
 The kids at school called pomegranates Chinese Apples
& divvied up bubblegum cigarettes which we blew into

pushing sugary smoke into the wind. I wanted
    to be like my father
because I loved my mother, so I learned how to handle

cards & studied him as he smoked & crooned
    Strangers in the Night as he drove
Brooklyn streets, bringing me home to her house,

a Mets game between innings on the radio. From
    my place in the backseat how could I have saved
any of us? How could I have known what to save?

Virgil Suárez

Cosas Sinatra

My father believed the streets of Spain to be clean,
the civil police in rare form as they stood straight
and saluted when asked a question, or for directions,
lost dogs, etc. I ate my first apple, actually more like a dozen,
and ended up with *un empacho* as my mother

called a stomach upset, ate grapes, cheese, liqueur-
filled bonbons, potato chips, sardines, oysters. . . .
Saw the snow fall one year, these flecks as if out
of torn pillow, idyllic stuff. Oh, flew kites
from our twelve-story apartment balcony,

rode the elevators as a prank to the *portero*,
who unbeknownst to me at the time kept his eyes
on German nudie magazines, flashes of pink to me,
who couldn't care less if I ran up the stairs.
Watched John Wayne movies with my father

at the Candileja's Sunday matinee. *The Guns
of Navarone* and *Cowboys* two of my father's favorites,
and I would say mine too, for we watched them fourteen
Sundays that one year. Nothing bad, I confess,
nothing like what made those German soldiers

in the movie put their hands to their ears every time
the huge guns blasted a shell at the ships on the horizon.
Played soccer at the park, the pinball machines
when I went to the bars with my father, who loved
gambas al ajillo, fried *chorizo*, and tap beer. *Serrano* ham

too, all that cholesterol food that turned our cheeks
red. My father's Spanish friends called it *fortaleza*,
this ability to line one's stomach with good food
and good wine. If the place had a jukebox, my father
put in coins and played the songs he liked and found

by Nat King Cole, Matt Monro, and Frank Sinatra—
most of the time it was Sinatra though, whom he loved,
and I remember the pinball machines and how when
I coaxed them the wrong way, they shut off and flashed
TILT and I didn't know what it meant, and my father

said that tilt meant what Sinatra did on stage when
his elegant, slim body moved real suave, cool, and his hands
and fingers shook to the beat of each note and he had
this way of turning, and I figured it mostly meant
that I was having too much fun and then I'd pull the plug

to reset the machine and my father gave me more money
to start playing all over again, and when the machine
went quiet one more time, I heard my own breathing rise
before the music coming from the corner, always the corner
of those smoky, penumbra-ridden bars where my father drank

with his friends, and then I would walk home, numb
in the cold, hands deep inside my empty pockets,
to tell my mother my father would be home as soon
as the songs ended and he drank the rest of his beer,
and I thought of nothing more, just the wind, cold,

the way the old men sagged in their overcoats on park
benches, the way my feet ached and the blisters on my
fingers hurt from playing so much pinball when I should
have been doing my homework, and on the way I learned
all those songs Sinatra sang and that my father loved;

the snow fell quietly and settled on everything,
like sepia dust fallen backwards from the heavens,
like these memories that have found a final, quiet form
on a leaden sky, when everyone was alive and happy
no matter the weather, and even the snow seemed content

to find its way to the earth, in Madrid, Spain,
from the years 1970 to 1974, lingered in the air
long enough for a father to speak about music,
la reconciliación de todas las cosas Sinatra,
after so many years, for a father, for a son.

Daniel Donaghy

Felix and the School Desk

He found it in his dumpster,
drawers gone, paint chipped,
curses carved into the desktop.
"A little project," he said,
winking at my brother and me
on our way to shoot hoops,
sandpaper and plywood
tucked under his good arm.
Evenings he'd put George
behind the bar and get back
to the storage room,
whistling Frank Sinatra
while he rebuilt the drawers
then sanded every inch,
"Angel Eyes," "What's New?"
"It's a Lonesome Old Town,"
my brother and me watching
through the basement window
while he thumbed the inkwell
smooth, the pencil gutter,
and beneath the handles,
gliding up and down each leg,
his wife dead ten years,
his daughter trying to find
herself dancing topless in Jersey,
his hands turning raw,
dust everywhere, hacking cough,
realizing too late
he should have worn a mask,
still hawking phlegm into a napkin
when he kicked our fathers out,
still whistling Sinatra after last call,
"the wee small hours of the morning"
he'd tell us later, "when all

good children should be in bed,"
calling us in the next afternoon
to give us the school desk,
three coats of chestnut varnish,
a matching chair.
We'd have the world on a string,
he said, if we studied hard,
asking again if we liked it,
if we were sure we could carry it home,
telling us to make him proud.

Jack Ridl

The Drywallers Listen to Sinatra
While They Work

This morning, my mother, here
for the holidays, is washing
the breakfast dishes, when Al, wiry,
coated with drywall dust takes
her hand and says, "I bet you loved
Sinatra. Dance?" The acrid smell
of plaster floats through the room.
Frank is singing, "All or nothing
at all," and Al leads my mother
under the spinning ballroom lights
across the new sub-floor. He
is smiling. She is looking over
his shoulder. The other guys
turn off their sanders. Al
and my mother move through
the dust, two kids back
together after the war. Sinatra
holds his last note. "It's been
seven years since I danced,"
my mother says. "Then
it was in the kitchen, too."
Al smiles again, says,
"C'mon then, Sweetheart!"
biting off his words like the ends
of the good cigars he carries
in his pocket. Sinatra's singing
"My Funny Valentine" and
my mother lays her hand in Al's.
They dance again, she looking
away when she catches my eye,
Al leading her back
across the layers of dust.

Jill Bialosky

Fathers in the Snow
Part Two

After father died
the love was all through the house
untamed and sometimes violent.
When the dates came we went up to our rooms
and mother entertained.
Frank Sinatra's "Strangers in the Night,"
the smell of Chanel No.5 in her hair and the laughter.
We sat crouched at the top of the stairs.
In the morning we found mother asleep on the couch
her hair messed, and the smell
of stale liquor in the room.
We knelt on the floor before her,
one by one touched our fingers
over the red flush in her face.
The chipped sunlight through the shutters.
It was a dark continent
we and mother shared;
it was sweet and lonesome,
the wake men left in our house.

David Cappella

One Tough Dame

The woman I left my wife for
told me one afternoon
that she hated Frank Sinatra.
"I hate him and his music.
He can't sing at all.
That stuff is old hat."

Just like that. There I was.
Smack dab alone, reeling
in the late night honky-tonk
blue haze of doubt, a tough place
to sit and have a drink
with your heart. Not for Frank.

A tough dame, the heart;
she wants top shelf, a cigarette,
and, baby, some attention.
And The Voice gave it
to her. Like a fine drink,
it soothed life's sleaze

with silky breath that smoothes
as easily as it jilts. "Oh honey,"
every phrase says, "I won't break you.
Lemme buy you one more, please.
Come on, a doll like you?"
Only Frank buys the heart a third drink.

But, damn, he hit a stonewall
with my woman. He saw class,
a real good broad. He didn't know
she was tone-deaf and tight
to his late-night notes which fell
at her feet, smoked-out butts.

"Sinatra, what a joke," she spat out.
A tough nut, this one, so I shrugged.
Then I applied the easy plead,
the coaxing "Aw, come on now?"
But, it's no use, she hates him –
every damn song, every damn note.

When she left me, I gulped a shot,
and listened to Frank. He said it all.
He knew the score with women.
He knew romance, how it fell like dice.
Frank never ditched me, never
let the hurt muscle out the hope.

Thomas Michael McDade

Young Guy Singing Sinatra
For Gary Edwards

Gary knew hundreds of songs,
and worked a Village corner
where he once found a Rolex
in his guitar case
among the bills, change,
sticks of gum, cigarettes
and the tears
of a South African man
who'd cried listening to
"Blowin' in the Wind."
Old-timers liked Gary's hat,
never dreamed a fedora
could look so good
on long hair.
They loved hearing
a young guy sing Sinatra.
Gary claimed he was happier
than a fly in a fart factory
playing that corner,
which didn't stop him
from finally leaving
to join a law firm.
He cut off his ponytail,
tucked it in a dresser drawer
among socks and handkerchiefs.
As for the fedora,
it still worked.
Old fans regularly
stopped him in the street.
And settled
for Sinatra *a capella*.

Peter Bethanis

American Future

In 1963 the morning probably seemed harmless enough
to sign on the dotted line as the insurance man
talked to my parents for over an hour
around a coffee table about our future.
This roof wasn't designed to withstand meteors
he told my father, who back then had a brush haircut
that made his ears stick out, his moods
still full of passion, still willing to listen,
my mother with her beehive hairdo,
smiling back at him, all three of them
wanting so much to make the fine print
of the world work. They laughed
and smoked, and after they led the man
politely to the door, my parents returned
to the living room and danced in the afternoon light,
the phonograph playing Frank Sinatra,
the green Buick's payments up to date,
five-hundred dollars safely in the bank—
later that evening, his infallible common sense
ready to protect us from a burst pipe or dry rot,
my father waded up to his ankles in water,
a V of sweat on the back of his shirt.
Something loomed deeper than any basement
on our block, larger than he was,
a fear he could not admit was unsolvable
with a monkey wrench or a handshake and a little money down.

David Lehman

January 20

When Robert Frost recited "The Gift Outright"
in the gleaming cold noonday sun I was watching
there was no school I don't remember why
that afternoon we played touch football, my friends and I
on a sloping meadow in Fort Tryon Park
and life was going on elsewhere, life was going on downtown
in the night clubs that even then were going out of fashion
like the Stork Club or El Morocco and my friends and I
wanted to grow up and smoke cigarettes and drink highballs
and buy fur coats for our wives and take them to clubs
because that was life, and what we didn't realize
was that our afternoon in Fort Tryon Park
where we got into a fight with some Irish kids
was also life and even then was turning
into history with the Bay of Pigs and the Vienna Summit
and Berlin and the missile crisis and the speech in Berlin
and the discotheques that put the night clubs out of business
and Sam Giancana, the mob boss who would've
ordered a hit on Sinatra except he wanted
to hear him sing "Chicago" one more time

Chris Clement

Sinatra
(An Epic Poem)

The city of White Trash, New York,
Town of tribulation without end,
Once peaceful and good, no trouble,
Taking control, now city of evil,
Not because of the people, only this reason:
A god-forsaken cult, terrorizing all,
Troublesome tribulation to them.
The pain-leaving leader, Brute Boyache,
Taking individuals, innocent,
Making them guilty, forcing them to do
His vile works. Stealing, killing,
Pushing the city, falling city, to its end...

Crooner at a local tavern, casual, cool,
Basics to say for himself, nothing more.
Known as Frankie Baby, Old Blue Eyes, Frank Sinatra.
Seeing all around as persecutions partake
Of these people right before his eyes,
Frankie is filled with a new song,
And vows to all that he will clean the place.
As he speaks, another, bloodthirsty, brainwashed,
Attempts to do him in once more.
Frank, filled now with power beyond explanation,
Hurls sick man through the window of the
Balcony above the stage with one swift blow...

The cult, full of evil and ready to harm,
Sits in the old abandoned skyscraper,
Making a plot, smoking their pot,
Knowing not of their new rival.
He seeks to find them, destroy them.
Out of nowhere their numbers appear,
Seeking to destroy Frank again.

One lays a hand on him and is scorched on contact.
Screaming with fear, he tries to run.
Frankie jumps, far and high, landing in front,
Preventing escape by the neck, snapping it
Like a toothpick between his nerved fingers…

The wrecked skyscraper in the heart of
White Trash knows not of its fate.
But Frankie is here, seeking them that harm.
No more will they rule.
Dark building, many stairs, new man of fame,
On his way up, killing any who confront him.
Top floor, darker than the lightless sky,
Is center of evil. But Frank has come.
He bursts through the door. Big table before him,
Only one at the head: Brute.
Frankie leaps as the bullets ring from a Tommy gun.
The super singer lands on the table running at
Top speed, kicks his foe square in the jaw,
Causing cracking and tearing as blood begins to pour.
Old Blue Eyes now takes down the building,
With defeated cult inside, fulfilling his vow,
And White Trash comes together to celebrate
Frank Sinatra.

E.J. Thribb (284)

In Memoriam Frank Sinatra

So. Farewell then.
Frank Sinatra.

In your Song,
New York, New York,
You said you wanted
To be

Top of the List
And
King of the Hill.

Perhaps you weren't
Aware that
These positions had already
Been filled.

By Ben Nevis
And Hamish Brown
Respectively.

Bernard Kennedy

Old Blue Eyes

He was hungry for dinner at eight,
and swaggered onto the music stage,
with audiences eager for song,
and presence of the confident master of
control,
in life and film and legend.
From black-haired youth to grey old man,
a colossus, who could
make it there and anywhere,
it was up to him.

Women's love filled that need
of affection and
men the saloon chums,
song gathered the eyes of
the blue sea of admiration,
from sixty years,
through cinema and song.

When your awaited death
broke on sky,
the tributes recalled
everybody's years,
everybody's emotions and
romantic loves,
the heart of living,
fantasy and romance
were statued by you.
Your tuxedo approach to life
sealed those moments in
the acceptable world,
no longer private,
and that's life.

You were puppet, pauper,
and King of the Hill,
and living was underlined as
your way, and looking death
as a contract on you,
and you at the bar, to look
in the eye,
The Grim Reaper.

Put away the calendar, the vinyl,
the magazines and fashion,
hang up the tuxedo,
sink the Daniels and Camel,
and start all over again.
The bar is now closed,
the concert hall empty,
the tributes all over,
so long saloon man,
adios amigos,
Hollywood, take down your sign,
and Blue Eyes,
shine,
in the Big Casino.

Joseph Stanton

In the Wee For Sinatra Small Hours

Look at yourself, you voice, so very glad
to be unhappy, though unrequited love's
a bore, and you've got it pretty bad,

and you can't get along without her,
no, not really very well, though you try
and try to be so glad to be unhappy

and smile long notes through a mood indigo,
your blues so cool, holding the smiling whiskey
of your aging vibrato, swirled in the glass

of unrelenting style, deep in a dream
of some sort of her we've all lost, too, with you
seeing all our losses, as if you were singing

somehow all our sorrows, every life we've
wept tearless in the wee small hours, mourning
with a smile and a last, long curl of smoke,   adrift.

Maria Mazziotti Gillan

My Funny Valentine

When I think of My Funny Valentine, I think of the boy I
loved in college and the juke box in the student center that
played whatever we wanted if only we put a quarter in. I'd
hear Sinatra's song and dream about this boy who took me
out but never kissed me, except once, with his thin mouth
closed and his arms
and body not touching mine in the back of Bill
Klangdorfer's father's Buick. He was skinny
with a kind of electric energy that radiated
out of his body and black horn-rimmed glasses
and the movements of an out-of-control marionette, his thin
face and dark small eyes, his black hair, straight and
already going sparse. I loved him.

He was my funny valentine and we worked
on the newspaper together—he doing the layout
and I writing the stories. I had all I could do to keep from
reaching out to touch his face, his hair.
I was always nervous around him, a sexual tension between
us that both of us were too scared and shy to touch, the
hours we spent together precious as pictures painted
carefully in a book, this boy I loved and cherished and
admired, this boy whose delicate, intelligent, monkey face I
still remember, though I haven't seen him in forty years,
and the way that song, Sinatra's beautiful, sorrowful voice,
always calls him up for me like a genie rising from a bottle.

Frank Van Zant

Sinatra 5.15.98

The scientist James Maxwell predicted that radio waves
would exist in space in a kind of forever.

From earth, 1956 bounces against Pluto
on its way to Andromeda,
1968 tangles with 1986, jangling
in the asteroid belt.

This is to say that after the final private O
of Sinatra's mouth, this crystal globe
will radiate his songs/our lives
once again, in a kind of forever:

teenagers will swoon, ancient as Sirens,
and his circle-breath notes will rise
like smoke rings from a mournful lover.

Ravi Shankar

The Day Sinatra Died
(After Frank O'Hara)

It is nearly 1:50 in New York a Thursday
Dante Alighieri and George Lucas' birthday,
anniversary of the day Jamestown was settled,
yes and it is not last call, not in the self-
proclaimed center of the world where the gas
is poured till the slivery moon is closer to light
than dark and I'm boxed in by finks who think
they're big-leaguers when the game's wiffle-ball,
pawing their cell phones and high-fiving,
and wouldn't it have been perfect if the Voice
came on the jukebox and a busload of bobbysoxers
poured in, but no, this is real life, 1998, and I'm holding
a watered down vodka tonic in a haze of smoke,
and there're no screws wearing suits with fabric
finer in the lining than upon slim lapels, no crooning,
no louche swagger or clacking of billiard balls,
hardly a soul carrying a Zippo and a roll of dimes,
and I will finish my drink, walk down the Avenue
of the Americas to the A/C/E line running local,
moving slower than I should, in synchronicity
with cabs idling curbside and across the Hudson,
Hoboken, which I can't see, glittering languidly,
one might even say, except for this fact of real life,
in a pose of mourning, pouring wave after wave
of brass and bel canto from here, where I will head
home, a little sad for no reason I can name, to eternity—

Jeremy Reed

Lyricists

Cole Porter sips a Harvey Wallbanger,
thumbing the song-sheets pinned by an ashtray
out on the breezy terrace. Rhyme by rhyme
the epic theme's miniaturized –

a Tolstoy novel got in 40 lines
with such hooky immediacy
the phrasing hangs in on a summer's day
and sticks a lifetime in the listener's mind.

The art talks up inconsequential things
as undercover poetry,
mooded by how a man in purple shoes
read life as melismatic journeyings,

its lesions and sweet cherry on the top.
He tilts a clipped fedora's brim
as fog soaks on the Pacific,
dry-icing with its fluffy lexicon.

A generation defined by its song,
it's more the ambient vocabulary
by which we live, Sinatra bending notes,
invoking midnight as he starts to sing

'Autumn in New York' or 'Foggy Day.'
The lyricist flavours the century,
alerting age to youth again.
He raps out chopstick percussion. His friend

walks naked to the bathroom. Time zips by.
A concentrated sonic feedback roar
builds on the grip of things, the summer day
is blasted to the back of a blue sky.

Charles O. Hartman

Anthem

I remember Bird, I remember
Clifford, I remember Django.
I remember you.

Says my heart, What is this thing
Called love? My foolish heart. People –
People will say we're in love, say it
Over and over again; it's the talk
Of the town. Who knows? How am I
To know? How about you? In your own
Sweet way, you don't know what
Love is, what a difference
A day made, what's new, what now,
My love. What is there to say?
I hear music. The song is you.

Where is love? In the middle
Of a kiss, on the sunny side of the street?
In the still of the night, in Tunisia?
Autumn in Washington Square?
Somewhere over the rainbow? Back
In your own back yard, on Broadway, Tuxedo
Junction, my state, my Kansas, my home?
I hear America singing; the song is you.
I'll remember April in Paris,
Evening in Paris, afternoon
In Paris – I love Paris, deed I do.
So what? I want to be
Where you are. I remember you.

Some other time, will you still
Be mine? Perhaps after all,
After you've gone there'll be
Other times; someday, sweetheart, *someday*
My prince will come, someone

To watch over me. Let's call this Look
For the Silver Lining. But not for me:
If some of these days I let a song
Go out of my heart, I'll never be the same.
There'll never be another you, just
A memory, yesterday's dreams, ghosts
Of yesterday. Yesterday
I didn't know about you, I didn't know
What time it was; my heart
Stood still. Ask me now, what kind
Of fool am I? Now's the time. I can't
Stop loving you; I can't pretend I can't
Believe that you're in love with me – I know
That you know how my heart sings.

You're my everything. How long
Has this been going on? Always
It's the same old story: out of nowhere
It could happen to you, all over again.
Everything happens to me – all
The things you are, my favorite things;
All of you, all of me; all day long, all through
The night; all too soon, too close
For comfort, too marvelous for words. All
Or nothing at all. Sometimes
I'm happy, sometimes I feel
Like a motherless child – but
Beautiful, careful, falling grace, bouquet,
Bewitched body and soul. Come
Rain or come shine, we'll be
Together, we'll be together
Again, again, time after time, moment
To moment, cheek to cheek.
Close your eyes, I'll close my eyes.
I feel a song coming on. The song is you.

Gerald Early

Listening to Frank Sinatra

As a boy, when you entered the tent,
Darkened and wet, like your childhood,
You kept straining to see, around or
Through the adults who were there;

You thought it smelled worse than any
Place you'd been before, and so you strained
Not to smell and you strained to see as
They paraded out, a sorry lot they were, too:

A grossly fat woman, a man with scaly skin,
Someone with a body like a tube, someone
With an appetite for glass and nails, and,
Last, a man with a bag over his head, a

Plain, brown, ordinary bag that everyone,
Waiting in hope, thought concealed behind
The horror of horrors, the most grotesque
Of the grotesque: he was your star that day.

With one sharp intake of breath, the shudder
Of utter joy that you were not, at last, this
Junk heap, we saw his face and wondered, this?!
And as he told his story, someone asked, jokingly,

What do you do all day? And he said, smiling,
Why, listen to Frank Sinatra, as if that was,
As if everyone should or would do what was
Naturalest thing in the whole wide natural world,

Reclining somewhere after work to listen
To "At Long Last Love," or "You Make Me Feel
So Young," or something else that helps
Get you through another day of just living.

And then you thought later, what could he know
Of Frank Sinatra, of sitting with a girl in
A darkened room, kissing wet kisses; driving
Along a dark, wet road with the hum of the radio.

But when you left the filthy tent that day
It was all you could remember, all you thought
Of, even after you forgot the face of horrors:
Listening to Frank Sinatra gets you through a day.

Ahhhh, such a story I like to tell my children
When we go out to tents and shows and sideshows
And I keep straining to hear Frank Sinatra off
Somewhere on a PA or someone's radio and they,

My children, always staring, wondering why
Their father is the crazy one who wants to
Hear Frank Sinatra where there is no Frank Sinatra,
Where no one else wants to hear Frank Sinatra at all.

To which looks I reply that if Frank Sinatra could
Do so much for the man who was the horror of horrors,
To sing such that he could make it through a day
Just think what such listening can do for me.

Diane Raptosh

Parts of Speech

The silent night of the flesh has been a journey toward
the rightness of another human face: the knowing loin of
the noise; the mouth, in its successive lapses toward the
sea. The cranium's base arcs a small heaven. From low
in its crib, muscled and mucous, buzzes the larynx like
so many leaf cutter ants. The light plum taste of forming
vowel sounds is a go at freedom; the cicada's screech
levers a charley horse to the throat. As does crying in a
dream. But here is what's really at issue. At the end of
every word that called for one, for mostly every note
Sinatra forged and held—long as rue and pure as catkin
fluff: his clean pronunciation of the consonant.

Postscript

I've Heard that Song Before...

The screensaver on my office computer at Central Connecticut State University is a photo of Frank Sinatra and then-wife Mia Farrow arriving at Truman Capote's famous 1966 "Black and White Ball," the so-called "Party of the Century." Lining my office walls are a five-foot-high Sinatra/Columbia Records CD display from Borders; a 1949 MGM "family portrait" with Sinatra buried in the fourth of five rows between Ginger Rogers and Red Skelton; a poster for the 1966 Kirk Douglas film *Cast a Giant Shadow*, with "special appearances by Frank Sinatra, Yul Brynner, and John Wayne;" and sundry smaller items, including a 1946 Sinatra endorsement of a "self-charging portable radio" from General Electric; postcards of Dean Martin and Frank's second wife, Ava Gardner; and a Greek T-shirt featuring Socrates, Plato, and Frank. There are also more than two shelves of Sinatra-related books. Amidst all of this, however, are my *other* books – on neo-Latin poetry; the American Puritan writers Cotton Mather, Edward Taylor, and Anne Bradstreet; and the late 18th-Century literary circle the Connecticut Wits. During the few moments of quiet that I enjoy in the office, the metaphysical questions raised by Talking Heads' 1981 "Once in a Lifetime" not infrequently come to mind: How'd I get here? My God, what have I done?

I could blame it on Rio because it was Sinatra's 1946 recording of "The Coffee Song (They've Got an Awful Lot of Coffee in Brazil)" that began my collection, when in the late seventies I purchased my first Sinatra album for $1.99, a reissue of *Frank Sinatra's Greatest Hits: The Early Years Volume I*, at Record Theatre in Norwood, Ohio, where I was working in a Cincinnati chili parlor. I simply couldn't refuse such a swingin' song on the perils of surplus resources. Economics with a rhythm section, how could I go wrong?

I could blame my Italian-American parents who, while never buying his records, nevertheless made the singer a household presence by faithfully watching his television specials, such as "The Main Event – Live from Madison Square Garden" (1974) and "Sinatra and Friends" (1977), which contains my most vivid small-screen Sinatra memory: Frank, Dean, and opera star Robert Merrill whooping it up on Frank Loesser's "The Oldest Established (Permanent Floating Crap Game in New York)."

I could even blame John Denver, one of my earliest favorites, who on his 1976 album *Spirit* introduced me to "Polka Dots and Moonbeams," which I would later discover to be one of my favorite Sinatra-Dorsey recordings. In that same year, ABC aired *John Denver and Friend* with the folk singer and you-know-who, and I was watching.

Yet, even given what many might consider embarrassing confessions of my juvenile, if not simply poor, musical taste, nothing here yet explains how I ended up in the office described above. Nor does it begin to account for my two books, *A Storied Singer: Frank Sinatra as Literary Conceit* (2002) and the one you are holding. These I can blame on graduate school.

My research asked some basic questions: Why would anyone choose to write in the language of Virgil, Horace, and Ovid in what they all believed to be a brand new world? Didn't a reactionary tool like neo-Latin contradict the boundless future that America seemingly offered from the beginning of European settlement? What was it that attracted Puritan writers like Cotton Mather and Samuel Sewall to it? For the answers, see my page-turning dissertation, *"Musae Americanae*: The Neo-Latin Poetry of Colonial and Revolutionary America," 1992.

Looking back, I can see that the qualities that drew me to neo-Latin are the very ones that had first fascinated me about Sinatra's interpretations of the

"Great American Songbook." For Berlin, Kern, Porter, Gershwin and Gershwin, Rodgers and Hart, and Styne and Cahn were among the songwriters who, within the confines of Tin Pan Alley, had to find repeated ways of saying something fresh, something smart, something (dare I say?) classic about the same old thing. These songs, after all, are not about innovation in form, style, or theme; they're about "saying 'I Love You' in 32 bars," as the old saying goes. And the only question facing the lyricist was how to tackle it this time around.

Frank Sinatra, as he took fuller control of his career at Capitol Records in the 1950s, and, with arranger Nelson Riddle and producer Voyle Gilmore, began to exploit fully the thematic possibilities of the long-playing record, looked back to these songs and reclaimed them. And more than any other twentieth-century singer, he truly made them his own. One need only note that, despite his receiving co-writing credit on but a handful of lesser-known recordings, the "Sinatra Song" has become a genre of its own, the subject of dozens of tribute albums and even a few radio stations. Why? Because his recording of a standard sounds so much like they are his words that it never seems quite right sung by anybody else.

Of course, I am far from the first to note this about Sinatra and certainly will not be the last to write about him. What sets my research apart, however, is its literary emphasis. Sinatra the man interests me far less than what writers have made of him – and done with/to him. I prefer exploring an author's creation and (ab)use of a multitude of "Frank Sinatras." This anthology, for example, offers wonderful poetry in which the cultural, social, political, and personal aspects of Sinatra resonate powerfully. To the poets, he's not simply an American pop culture icon, he's hope, fear, anger, success, disappointment, democracy, empire....

Thus, if my office seems as overstuffed as 1940s Brazil was with coffee beans, it's due to my sharing it with so many Franks: not only "The Voice," "Ol' Blue

Eyes," and "The Chairman of the Board," but also the political symbol and commercial product. Appropriately, perhaps the multiplicity of Sinatra is best captured by a 1702 neo-Latin anagram on "Cottonus Matherus" by John Danforth:

> *Tu tantum cohors es.*
> You alone are an army.

Gilbert L. Gigliotti

Notes on the Introduction and Poems

Introduction
The rhymes "Sumatra," "martyrs," "mantra," and "Sartre" are taken from the following songs, respectively: "I'd Rather be with You" (Doris Day and Johnny Parker with Les Brown, 1945); "Deportees Club" (Elvis Costello and the Attractions, 1984); "Sinatra Mantra" (Victim's Family, 1995); and "Had Away, Gan On" (Jez Lowe and the Bad Pennies, 1998).

Consider the ubiquity of "My Way" in news reports from around the world: A military band's playing it at the request of German Chancellor Gerhard Schröder for his official retirement ceremony (*Spiegel Online* 11/21/05); its status as the most popular secular song at British funerals (*Mail and Guardian Online* 11/18/05); Slobodan Milosevic's favoring it while awaiting his genocide trial in his cell at the Hague (*Harper's Weekly Review* 2/12/02); and the song's strange relationship with the people of the Philippines – both inspiring Filipino troops in Iraq (*Global Nation*, 11/03) and sparking repeated violence at karaoke bars in Manila (*TaipeiTimes.com* 11/06/05).

Trilogy spent 12 weeks and reached number 17on the *Billboard* Album Chart in 1980, was nominated for six Grammy Awards, and won one. And its critical and commercial success proved that, in fact, we still needed and apparently were still willing to feed him, when he was sixty-four.

The Sex Pistols
Sinatra's own dislike of the song is well-documented, and even as he would perform it in concert his antipathy toward it could be sensed in such introductions as the one on 1974's *The Main Event*, with the opening

chords playing: "We will now do the National Anthem, but you needn't rise…" Reed's imagery reflects well the mellifluousness of the classical *bel canto* tradition in which Henry Pleasants, in his 1974 *The Great American Popular Singers*, argues Sinatra worked (189).

Obituary
According to www.GeorgeGerdes.com, Gerdes's label, United Artists, would not risk the legal repercussions of using Frank Sinatra as a character in the poem so the final three lines were revised to: "…Folk hero George Gerdes, who once met Joe back in 1967, summed up Reissler's entire career by remarking, 'Adios.'"

Last Walk with Sinatra's Dog
These line numbers are taken from the 1996 translation of the *Odyssey* by Robert Fagles. The lines in the original Greek are 11.121-137.

Skylark
Much to many people's surprise and chagrin, "Skylark," the 1941 Johnny Mercer/Hoagy Carmichael standard was, in fact, never recorded by Sinatra. That both Ruth Foley and the poet of the previous poem, Greg Rappleye, imagine his singing it suggests much about Sinatra's intimate connection to the "Great American Songbook": if it's a great song, he must have sung it.

Sinatra
According to Robert Wrigley, the misnaming of the Sinatra character in the 1953 film *From Here to Eternity* was accidental (Sinatra played "Maggio" not "Prewitt"), but, even after he discovered it, he chose not to alter the line since the mistake fits the poem's addressee so well.

Had Away, Gan On
The cd booklet of the 1998 release by Jez Lowe and the Bad Pennies, *Parish Notices*, states the phrase is "a County Durham dialect expression meaning 'Get away, go on.'"

The Third Mirror Displacement
Robert Smithson (1938-1973) was an American artist whose work in a variety of fields (earthworks, sculpture, film, essay) was highly influential.

Reading Emily Dickinson
The poet's endnote in *The Gospel According to Frank* reads: "Arthur Miller and Marilyn Monroe were married from 1956 to 1961. Thomas Johnson's definitive edition of Emily Dickinson's *Collected Poems* appeared in 1955."

Sinatra Walks Out
The endnote in *The Emily XYZ Songbook* reads: "The B Voice (right column) contains actual quotes attributed to Frank Sinatra mostly concerning female reporters and journalists."

In Memoriam Frank Sinatra
E.J. Thribb (17 ½) is a fictitious poet, invented by the British satiric magazine *Private Eye*, whose name (and random parenthetical ages) is now synonymous with bad poetry.

Anthem
In form, this is a cento, a poem comprised entirely of lines from other poems. Hartman stitches together titles from the "Great American Songbook." Sinatra, whose recordings many view as having been essential to the formation of the canon, recorded no fewer than 36 of the titles used in this poem.

Index of Contributors with Poem Titles
and Composition Dates

Contributors

Peter Bethanis grew up in rural Maine and is currently an Assistant Professor of English at Ball State University. His poems and essays have appeared in over fifty literary journals including *Poetry*, *Tar River*, and the *Lullwater Review*. He has won the Eve of St. Agnes poetry award and has been a featured poet on *Poetry Magazine*'s website.

Grace Butcher retired (Emerita, English) from Kent State University Geauga Campus in '93 and is currently teaching creative writing at her alma mater, Hiram College. Her work is included in *The Best American Poetry 2000*, and her book *Child, House, World* won her the Ohio Poet of the Year award for books published in 1991. She is the editor of *The Listening Eye.*

Giovanna Capone writes poetry, fiction, autobiographical essays, and plays. Her writing has appeared in various books, including: *Unsettling America*, a multicultural poetry anthology; *The Voices We Carry: Recent Italian American Women's Fiction*; and *Bless Me, Father: Stories of Catholic Childhood*. She also has co-edited *Hey Paesan! Writing by Lesbians and Gay Men of Italian Descent.*

David Cappella is an Associate Professor of English at Central Connecticut State University. He is the co-author with Baron Wormser of *Teaching the Art of Poetry: The Moves* and of *A Surge of Language: Teaching Poetry Day to Day*. His chapbook, *Gobbo: A Solitaire's Opera*, won the 2004 Bright Hill Press Poetry Chapbook Competition, and the first poem in the sequence was nominated for a Pushcart Prize. His poems have appeared in *The Connecticut Review*, *Diner*, *The Bryant Literary Review*, *The Bradford Review* and other journals.

Christopher Clement's poem was written in 1997, "... originally as an assignment for a creative writing class my senior year in high school. I have been a big fan of

Frank Sinatra's music for quite a long time, at first listening with my Grandmother at a younger age. I am a musician with a very different style, but a great respecter of all genres. The day Frank Sinatra died I paid my respects with a weeklong marathon of his music from my record collection."

Daniel Donaghy's first collection of poems, *Streetfighting*, has just been published by BkMk Press. His poems have appeared or are forthcoming in such journals as *Prairie Schooner*, *New Letters*, *The Southern Review*, *Poet Lore*, *Cimarron Review* and *Texas Review*, and in the Summer 2001 issue of *Organica*. He has received fellowships from the National Endowment for the Humanities, the Constance Saltonsall Foundation for the Arts, and the Cornell Council for the Arts. He is Assistant Professor of English at Eastern Connecticut State University.

Francine DuBois and **Hezekiah Allen Taylor** are pseudonymns for Jennifer Heinecke and Kathleen Davis

Jacques Duvall and Alain Chamfort, according to *Le Nouvel Observateur*, "sometimes… produce songs that resemble the gallant paradoxes of a pagan Saint Augustine" And "if Sinatra is Jupiter, and Marvin Gaye is Apollo, then Chamfort is Cupid."

Gerald Early is a noted essayist and American culture critic. A professor of English, of African and Afro-American Studies, and of American Culture Studies, Early is the author of several books, including *The Culture of Bruising: Essays on Prizefighting.* He is also editor of numerous volumes, including *The Muhammad Ali Reader* (1998), *The Sammy Davis, Jr., Reader* (2001), and *Miles Davis and American Culture (2001)*. He served as a consultant on Ken Burns' documentary films on baseball and jazz, which both aired on PBS.

Landis Everson was born in 1926 in Coronado, California and was a member of the Berkeley Renaissance of the 1940s, which carried over into the San Francisco Renaissance of the 1950s, and his poems were printed in *Poetry*, *Hudson Review*, *Kenyon Review*, *Locus Solus*, and *Quarterly Review of Literature* before 1962. Forty-three years passed before Mr. Everson appeared in print again, during which time he was not writing poetry. Since being rediscovered in Ben Mazer's anthology of the Berkeley Renaissance in *Fulcrum* 3, Everson has written new poems which have appeared in *Poetry*, *The London Review of Books*, *The New Yorker*, *American Poetry Review*, *Fulcrum*, *The New Republic* and more than 30 other periodicals. In fall 2005 he became the first winner of the Poetry Foundation's Emily Dickinson Award for a poet over the age of 50 who has never published a book of poems.

Paul Fericano, a San Francisco native, is a poet, writer, and satirist. For more than thirty years his stand-up poetry and controversial satires have been brought to the public's attention mostly through the dedicated efforts of independent publishers and a loyal group of readers. He was editor/publisher of Scarecrow Books and Poor Souls Press. In 1980, he co-founded (with Elio Ligi) the first parody news and disinformation syndicate, Yossarian Universal News Service (YU), which the Los Angeles Times dubbed, "unbelievable news for unbelievable times."

Aaron Fogel's books include *The Printer's Error* (Miami UP, 2001), *Coercion to Speak: Conrad's Poetics of Dialogue* (Harvard UP, 1985), and Chain Hearings (Inwood/Horizon Press 1976). He teaches at Boston University.

Ruth E. Foley's poetry has appeared in over fifty journals and magazines, including "Hanging Loose," "RATTLE," and "Confrontation." She lives in southeastern Massachusetts where she works for a nonprofit adult literacy organization.

George Gerdes is a singer/songwriter/actor whose albums include *Obituary* and *Son of Obituary*, and who has appeared in such films as *Amistad* and *Single White Female* as well as such television programs as *Seinfeld*, *NYPD Blue*, and *The X Files*.

Dana Gerringer has been to a few schools, taken a few classes, and audited a few lives. She is a Euro-mutt siren who loves life, books about life, and listening to *This American Life* on NPR. She does her best to soak up everything she can by reading about it, living her own, and always taking notes along the way.

Kara L.C. Jones is a graduate of Carnegie Mellon University, actually walked in the Neighborhood of Make Believe, founded KotaPress after her son was stillborn, commits acts of henna on any body within reach, and recently began to blend her magic through www.HennaHealing.com started in 2003.

Maria Mazziotti Gillan is the founder and the executive director of the Poetry Center at Passaic County Community College in Paterson, NJ. She is also the director of the Creative Writing Program and a Professor of Poetry at Binghamton University-State University of New York . She has published eight books of poetry, including *Where I Come From.* She is co-editor of four anthologies, including *Unsettling America.* She is the editor of the *Paterson Literary Review.* Her work has appeared in *Prairie Schooner* and numerous other journals and anthologies. She has won, among other awards, the May Sarton Award and the American Literary Translator's Award through a grant from the National Endowment for the Arts.

Allen Ginsberg, 1926-1997, leading poet of the beat generation, is best known for *Howl.*

Beckian Fritz Goldberg holds an MFA from Vermont College and is the author of several volumes of poetry, *Body Betrayer* (1991), *In the Badlands of Desire* (1993), *Never Be the Horse* (1999), winner of the University of Akron Poetry Prize selected by Thomas Lux, and *Twentieth Century Children*, a limited edition chapbook, (1999). Her work has appeared widely in anthologies and journals including *The American Poetry Review, The Best American Poetry 1995, Field, The Gettysburg Review, Indiana Review, The Iowa Review, New American Poets of the 90's,* and *The Massachusetts Review*. She has been awarded the Theodore Roethke Poetry Prize, *The Gettysburg Review* Annual Poetry Award, The University of Akron Press Poetry Prize, and a Pushcart Prize. Her newest volume of poems, *The Book of Accident*, was published in 2006 by University of Akron Press. Currently, Goldberg directs the MFA Creative Writing Program at Arizona State University.

Charles O. Hartman, a Professor of English, Poet in Residence, Co-Director of Creative Writing at Connecticut College, has been publishing poetry for over three decades. He plays jazz guitar and has done critical writing on the relations between poetry and jazz and other musical forms, as well as on connections between poetry and computing, and on a variety of modern and contemporary poets.

Reuben Jackson works as an archivist with the Smithsonian Institution's Duke Ellington Collection. His poems have been published in 11 anthologies, and in a volume entitled "fingering the keys." He lives in Washington, D.C.

James Keelaghan is a Canadian singer-songwriter who has released nine albums, most recently *A Few Simple Verses* (2006).

Ruth Moon Kempher, of St. Augustine, Florida, owns Kings Estate Press and is the author of nineteen books of poetry. Her work appeared in the first issue of *Kalliope*, and she has been a respected contributor and supporter since.

Bernard Kennedy is a Priest of the Dublin Diocese, a poet, and psychoanalyst.

Ulf Kirchdorfer is Assistant Chair, Humanities, and Professor of English at Darton College. He has published poems in *Harvard Review*, *Poetry Daily*, *Christian Science Monitor*, *Mudfish, NY Quarterly*, and other.

Gerry LaFemina is the author of several collections of poetry including *The Parakeets of Brooklyn* (winner of the 2003 Bordighera Prize), *The Window Facing Winter*, and *Graffiti Heart* (winner of the 2001 MAMMOTH Books/ Anthony Piccione Prize in Poetry).

David Lehman David Lehman is the Series Editor of *The Best American Poetry Series*, and author of three books of poems, including *Valentine Place* (Scribner, 1996) and *Operation Memory* (Princeton, 1990). His prose books include *The Last Avant-Garde: The Making of the New York School of Poets*, *Signs of the Times: Deconstruction and the Fall of Paul de Man*, and *The Big Question*. He is on the core faculty of the graduate writing programs at Bennington College and the New School for Social Research. He divides his time between Ithaca, New York, and New York City. David Lehman is also the general editor of University of Michigan Press's Poets on Poetry Series.

Joel Lewis is longtime resident of Hoboken, where the Chairman remains a palpable presence. He is the author of *Vertical's Currency: New and Selected Poems* (Talisman House) and has edited an anthology of NJ poets, the selected talks of Ted Berrigan and the selected poems of Walter Lowenfels. Though not to be taken as a reflection of his baseline emotional state, his favorite Sinatra disks are the "Suicide albums" of his Capitol years.

Meg Kearney, author of *An Unkindness of Ravens* (BOA, 2001) and *The Secret of Me*, a young-adult novel in verse (Persea, 2005), was Associate Director of the National Book

Foundation in Manhattan for 11 years. She is now Director of the Solstice Creative Writing Programs of Pine Manor College in Massachusetts.

Lenny Lianne's poems have appeared in *Mudlark, Poet Lore, Tidepools, Phoebe* and are forthcoming in *Rattle, Epicenter, Poetry Motel* and *Hidden Oak* as well as several anthologies. Her poem "The Worst Lamb" received Honorable Mention in the 2003 Wergle Flomp Poetry Contest. She also has completed an unpublished poetry manuscript called "Past Point Comfort" about the beginning years of the Jamestown Colony.

David Lloyd directs the Creative Writing Program at Le Moyne College. In 2003 New American Press published his poem sequence *The Gospel According to Frank*. He is also the author of *Boys: Stories and a Novella* (Syracuse University Press, 2004); a poetry chapbook, *The Everyday Apocalypse*; a poetry anthology; and *The Urgency of Identity: Contemporary English-language Poetry from Wales*; and a collection of interviews, *Writing on the Edge: Interviews with Writers and Editors of Wales*. His articles, interviews, poems and stories have appeared in numerous magazines including *Colorado Review, Crab Orchard Review, Denver Quarterly, DoubleTake*, and *TriQuarterly*. In 2000, he received the Poetry Society of America's Robert H. Winner Memorial Award.

Jez Lowe, best known for his songs describing the mining culture, society and people of his native Northeast England, is a busy performer in high demand, with annual tours to the United States and Canada and frequent tours to Australia and New Zealand. Born to a coal mining family with Irish roots, Jez was raised and still lives in an area close to the English/Scottish border where coal mining was the dominant occupation.

Thomas Michael McDade lives in Monroe, Connecticut with his wife, Carol and works as a computer programmer. His poetry and short fiction have been published in many journals and reviews through the years.

Kelly Neill and the other members of Natasha's Ghost have written and produced five independent albums, including the critically acclaimed CDs *Everything Under The Moon* and *Shimmer*. In addition to garnering coast to-coast airplay on Alternative and Triple-A radio stations, songs from each of the group's recordings have been featured in independent films, major motion pictures and network television programs.

Kathleen Norris is the award-winning poet, writer, and author of The New York Times bestsellers, *The Cloister Walk*, *Dakota: A Spiritual Geography*, *Amazing Grace: A Vocabulary of Faith*, and *The Virgin of Bennington*. She has published seven books of poetry. Her first book of poems was entitled *Falling Off* and was the 1971 winner of the Big Table Younger Poets Award.

Sam Pereira's books include *The Marriage of the Portuguese, Brittle Water*, and *A Café in Boca*. His poetry has also appeared in such magazines as *American Poetry Review, Antioch Review, Missouri Review* and *Poetry*. He teaches in the California public school system, where he is forced to undergo almost daily reminders that none of his students has a clue as to the greatness of the artist, Sinatra.

Laurence Petit is an Assistant Professor of Contemporary British Literature at Central Connecticut State University. She is the author of several articles on text and image in the fiction of Anita Brookner and A.S. Byatt. A native of France, she is also a free-lance translator. Her translations include articles by Georges Bataille and Pierre Bourdieu, as well as a Globetrotter's Pocket Doc *Medical Handbook for Travelers*.

Diane Raptosh has published three books of poems from Guernica Editions: *Just West of Now* (1992), *Labor Songs* (1999), and *Parents from Another Alphabet* (2008). She holds the Eyck Berringer Chair in the English Department at Albertson College of Idaho.

Greg Rappleye's second book of poems, *A Path Between Houses*, (University of Wisconsin Press, 2000) won the Brittingham Prize. More recent work has appeared in *Poetry*, *The Southern Review*, and *Virginia Quarterly Review*. He lives near Grand Haven, Michigan.

Jeremy Reed From the Enitharmon Website: "He has published many volumes of poetry, as well as a *Selected Poems* (Penguin), and he has received the Eric Gregory and Somerset Maugham Awards. He has translated Montale, Novalis and Cocteau, and written critical studies of Rimbaud, de Sade and Lautréamont. Reed is also a noted writer on pop culture."

Jack Ridl's collection, *Broken Symmetry*, will be published in 2006 by Wayne State University Press. His *Against Elegies* was selected in 2001 by Sharon Dolin and Billy Collins for The Center for Book Arts Chapbook Award. Ridl is co-author with Peter Schakel of *Approaching Literature in the 21ˢᵗ Century* (Bedford/St. Martin's Press, 2005), and has had poems published in such literary journals as *Poetry*, *The Georgia Review*, *Ploughshares*, *Prairie Schooner*, and *The Denver Quarterly*.

Mary Ann Samyn is the author of four collections of poetry, most recently *Inside the Yellow Dress* and *Purr*, both from New Issues. Currently, she teaches in the MFA program at West Virginia University.

Matt Santateresa is a Canadian writer who lives in Montreal, Quebec, and has roots in New Haven, Connecti-cut. He has written three volumes of poetry and has appeared in numerous Canadian journals and periodicals. He is presently working on a fourth volume of poetry and a play, and is researching a sequence on "The Voice."

Ravi Shankar is Associate Professor and Poet-in-Residence at Central Connecticut State University and the founding editor of the international online journal of the arts, *Drunken Boat*. His first book, *Instrumentality*, was named a finalist for the 2005 Connecticut Book Awards. His creative and critical work has appeared in *The Paris Review, Poets & Writers, Time Out New York, Blackbird*, among many other publications. He has served as a commentator for NPR and received fellowships from the MacDowell Colony and Atlantic Center for the Arts. He currently reviews poetry for the *Contemporary Poetry Review*.

Robert Sheppard is Senior Lecturer in English and Creative Writing at Edge Hill College of Higher Education, UK, his *The Poetry of Saying: British Poetry and its Discontents 1950-2000* is published by Liverpool University Press. He has sung the blues in bands but his ambition to croon remains (publicly) unfulfilled. Favourite Sinatra album: Sinatra-Basie.

Joseph Stanton's poems have appeared in *Poetry*, *Poetry East*, *Harvard Review*, and many other journals. His books of poems include *Imaginary Museum: Poems on Art* (Time Being Books 1999) and *Cardinal Points: Poems on St. Louis Cardinals Baseball* (McFarland 2002). His latest book of essays is *The Important Books: Children's Picture Books as Art and Literature* (Scarecrow 2005). He teaches art history and American studies at the University of Hawaii at Manoa. He can be heard reading his Sinatra poem at www.cortlandreview.com.

Ruth Stone is the recipient of numerous honors, including the 2002 National Book Award, the National Book Critics Circle Award, the Cerf Lifetime Achievement Award for the state of Vermont, Guggenheim Awards, Pushcart Prizes, a Whiting Award, and the Shelley Memorial Award. She lives in Vermont.

Virgil Suárez was born in Havana, Cuba in 1962. He is the author of over twenty books of prose and poetry. His most recent book, *90 Miles: Selected and New*, is published by The University of Pittsburgh Press. He teaches at Bennington College and Florida State University and lives in Miami.

SuGar Yoshinaga is the lyricist, the guitarist, and a vocalist for *Buffalo Daughter*, the Japanese rock group formed with Yumiko Ohno on bass and MoOog Yamamoto on turn-tables.

Bruce Taylor's poetry, fiction and translations have appeared in such places as *The Chicago Review*, *The Exquisite Corpse*, *Light*, *The Nation*, *Nerve*, *The New York Quarterly*, *Poetry*, the *Vestal Review* and *E2ink-1: the Best of the Online Journals 2002*. Taylor has won awards and fellowships from the Bush Artist Foundation, Wisconsin Arts Board, the NEA, NEH, and Fulbright-Hayes.

David Trinidad's last two books, *Phoebe 2002: An Essay in Verse* and *Plasticville*, were published by Turtle Point Press. He teaches poetry at Columbia College in Chicago, where he directs the graduate poetry program and co-edits the journal *Court Green*.

Lawrence Upton has been making poetry for nearly four decades and is prolific in a variety of writing genres. In the mid 1970s he made text-sound composition at Fylkingen in Stockholm. Later, he was a member of "jgjgjg" and other performance groups and produced electro-acoustic pieces at West Square Studio. His collaboration and performance practice has persisted and developed, with many colleagues including Bob Cobbing, Jennifer Pike, and Alaric Sumner. Currently he is writing Bombing / Volvox / Multivoice. He has chaired Sub Voicive Poetry since 1994. He co-edited the anthology Word Score Utterance Choreography in Verbal and Visual Poetry (1998) with Bob Cobbing.

Frank Van Zant is the Director of Greenhouse, an alternative education program for students who need a second chance. He is the author of *Climbing Daddy Mountain* (Pudding House) and *The Lives of the Two-Headed Baseball Siren* (Kings Estate Press).

Robert Wrigley is the author of six books of poetry, most recently *Early Meditations, New and Selected Poems* (Penguin, 2006). He has also been awarded two Pushcart Prizes, two National Endowment for the Arts grants, a fellowship from the John Simon Guggenheim Memorial Foundation, and the Kingsley Tufts Award. He is an alumnus of Southern Illinois University Edwardsville.

Emily XYZ is a writer, performer and vocalist best known for her rhythmic poems for two voices. She first gained notice at New York's Nuyorican Poets Cafe in the 1990s, and her first recording, 1982's "Who Shot Sadat?" was named one of two "Indie Singles of the Year" in *The Village Voice*. The 2005 release of *The Emily XYZ Songbook* (Rattapallax Press) marks the first-ever publication of these works.

Acknowledgments

All poems are reprinted by the expressed permission of the authors.

Charles O. Hartman: *Anthem* from *Glass Enclosure* copyright © 1995 by Charles O. Hartman and reprinted by permission of Wesleyan University Press.

Jill Bialosky: *Fathers in the Snow* from *The End of Desire: Poems* copyright © 1997 by Jill Bialosky. Used by permission of Alfred A. Knopf, a division of Random House, Inc.

Kathleen Norris: *The Ignominy of the Living* from *Little Girls in Church* copyright © 1995. Reprinted by permission of the University of Pittsburgh Press.

E.J. Thribb (284): *In Memoriam Frank Sinatra* was first published in THE ANGRY CORRIE 37 (Jun-Jul 1998).

David Lehman: *January 20* is reprinted with the permission of Scribner, an imprint of Simon and Schuster Adult Publishing Group, from *The Evening Sun* copyright © 2002 by David Lehman.

Allen Ginsberg: *Las Vegas: Verses Improvised for El Dorado HS Newspaper* from *Collected Poems 1947-1980* Copyright © 1984 by Allen Ginsberg. Reprinted by permission of HarperCollins Publishers.

Gerald Early: *Listening to Frank Sinatra* is reprinted from *Prairie Schooner*, volume 63, number 3 (fall 1989) by permission of the University of Nebraska Press copyright 1989.

David Lehman: *March 16* is reprinted with the permission of Scribner, an imprint of Simon and Schuster Adult Publishing Group, from *The Daily Mirror* copyright © 2000 by David Lehman.

Bernard Kennedy: *Old Blue Eyes (Poem to Sinatra)* first appeared in *Autumn Leaves* (1998).

Robert Wrigley: *Sinatra* first appeared in *The Kenyon Review*, New Series, Fall 1989, Vol. IX, No. 3.

William Hathaway: *Why that's Bob Hope* is reprinted by permission of Louisiana State University Press from *Fish, Flesh, and Fowl* by William Hathaway copyright © 1985 by William Hathaway.

George Jessel: *Al Jolson (Asa Yoelson)* appeared in *Elegy in Manhattan* copyright © 1961, reprinted with the permission of Henry Holt and Compnay.

Peter Bethanis: *American Future* was first published in *Poetry* (vol. 174, no. 4).

Ruth Moon Kempher: *Fabulous Birds, the Rocs, etc.* appeared in *The Florida Education Journal* May 1966, and in *The White Guitar* Olivant Press, Homestead, FL, 1967, 2nd printing 1970.

Daniel Donaghy: *Felix and the School Desk* appeared in *Streetfighting* (BkMk 2000).

Joseph Stanton: *For Sinatra in the Wee Small Hours* appeared in *The Cortland Review* (www.cortlandreview.com).

Jez Lowe: *Had Away, Gan On* is reprinted with permission of Lowe Life Music. It originally appeared on the 1998 Jez Lowe and the Bad Pennies release *The Parish Notices* from Green Linnet Records.

Kelly Neill: *Hang Sinatra* is used with permission from Chessysongs (ASCAP) and was originally released on the 1995 Natasha's Ghost release *Everything Under the Moon* on FUA Records; Kelly Neill, words and music; Robert Westlind, music; Dan de la Isla, music.

David Lloyd: *The Heavens* and *Reading Emily Dickinson* are reprinted from *The Gospel According to Frank* New American Press 2003.

Giovanna Capone: *I Met Her in Front of the Tomato Sauce* appeared in the Spring 1996 issue of the on-line journal *Sapphic-Ink*.

David Trinidad: *Movin' with Nancy* is reprinted from *Hand over Heart* Amethyst Press 1991.

Diane Raptosh: *Neck and Neck* and *Parts of Speech* first appeared in *Terrain.org: A Journal of the Built and Natural Environments* 12 (Fall/Winter 2002).

James Keelaghan: *Sinatra and I* appeared in *Home* copyright © 2001, reprinted with permission from Jericho Beach Music.

Ruth E. Foley: *Skylark* appeared in *Agnieska's Dowry* A Small Garlic Press.

Ruth Stone: *Schmaltz* appeared in *Ordinary Words* copyright © 1999, reprinted with permission from Paris Press.

Gilbert L. Gigliotti is Professor and Chair in the Department of English at Central Connecticut State University. A specialist in the classical influences on early American literature, he has taught courses on such Puritan writers as Cotton Mather, Anne Bradstreet, and Edward Taylor, as well as on Greek and Roman literature and the literature of Sinatra. He is the author *A Storied Singer: Frank Sinatra as Literary Conceit* (2002), has mounted several exhibits of his Sinatra memorabilia collection, lectures frequently on the singer, and hosts a weekly radio show on Tuesday mornings on WFCS 107.7 FM (New Britain and Hartford, Connecticut) and at www.wfcsradio.com. His wife cried more than he when Sinatra died, and his daughters are two of the very few of their generation to have seen 1943's *Ghosts on the Loose* with Ava Gardner, Bela Lugosi, Huntz Hall, and Leo Gorcey.

Made in the USA
Lexington, KY
21 January 2014